ST. MARTIN
&ST. BARTS
ALIVE

Harriet Greenberg & Douglas Greenberg

HUNTER

HUNTER PUBLISHING, INC.
130 Campus Drive, Edison, NJ 08818
732-225-1900; 800-255-0343; Fax 732-417-1744
hunterpub@emi.net

1220 Nicholson Road, Newmarket, Ontario
Canada L3Y 7V1
800-399-6858; Fax 800-363-2665

The Boundary, Wheatley Road, Garsington
Oxford, OX44 9EJ England
01865-361122; Fax 01865-361133

ISBN 1-55650-831-X
© 1999 Alive Travel Books, Ltd.

Maps by Kim André © 1999 Hunter Publishing, Inc.

About the Authors

Harriet Greenberg has been an avid world traveller and accomplished travel writer for over 20 years. She is the author of the award-winning *Israel On Your Own*, as well as other guides in the Alive series. She is currently researching *Puerto Rico Alive*, to be published next year.

Douglas Greenberg graduated from Arizona State University with a degree in Travel & Tourism. He works at Fox Sports in Los Angeles when he isn't exploring restaurants and nightlife on Caribbean islands.

About the Alive Guides

Reliable, detailed and personally researched by knowledgeable authors, the Alive series was founded by Harriet and Arnold Greenberg.

This accomplished travel-writing team also operates a renowned bookstore, **The Complete Traveller**, at 199 Madison Avenue in New York City.

Other titles in this series include: *Aruba, Bonaire & Curaçao Alive, Buenos Aires & The Best of Argentina Alive, Venezuela Alive, The Virgin Islands Alive,* and *Cancún & Cozumel Alive.*

www.hunterpublishing.com

Hunter's full range of travel guides to all corners of the globe is featured on our exciting web site. You'll find guidebooks to suit every type of traveler, no matter what their budget, lifestyle, or idea of fun. Full descriptions are given for each book, along with reviewers' comments and a cover image. Books may be purchased on-line using a credit card via our secure transaction system.

Alive Guides featured include: *Aruba, Bonaire & Curaçao, Buenos Aires & the Best of Argentina, Cancún & Cozumel Venezuela* and *The Virgin Islands*.

Check out our *Adventure Guides*, a series aimed at the independent traveler with a focus on outdoor activities (rafting, hiking, biking, skiing, etc.). All books in this signature series cover places to stay and eat, sightseeing, in-town attractions, transportation and more!

Hunter's *Romantic Weekends* series offers myriad things to do for couples of all ages and lifestyles. Quaint places to stay and restaurants where the ambiance will take your breath away are included, along with fun activities that you and your partner will remember forever.

Acknowledgements

To El Niño for the terrible weather that kept me indoors working on this book instead of at poolside working on my tan, and the great staff at The Complete Traveller who kept the bookstore running smoothly during my absences.

We Love to Get Mail

This book has been carefully researched to bring you current, accurate information. But no place is unchanging. We welcome your comments for future editions. Please write us at: *St. Martin & St. Barts Alive*, c/o Hunter Publishing, 130 Campus Drive, Edison, NJ 08818, or e-mail your comments to kimba@mediasoft.net.

Preface

Saint Martin/Sint Maarten, St. Barts and Anguilla are clustered at the northern tip of the Lesser Antilles island chain. Saint Martin/Sint Maarten, the largest and most populous island, is at the heart of this exclusive trio, with tiny St. Barts only 20 miles south and Anguilla even closer to the northeast. You can make your base on one of these islands and take leisurely daytrips to its neighbors.

Not simply land blips in a sea of blue, these islands have personalities defined by their former colonial rulers and by the mix of their current inhabitants. St. Barts and a large chunk of Saint Martin are French, both in spirit and ambiance. They offer the Caribbean's best restaurants, topless beaches and exclusive shops. The smaller but more developed Sint Maarten is Dutch, and most closely resembles St. Thomas in the US Virgin Islands. It has the largest number of duty-free shops in the Caribbean, high-rise resort hotels, gambling casinos and a golf course. The beaches of British Anguilla stretch for miles with ankle-deep white sand and off-shore coral reefs waiting to be explored by novice snorkelers and scuba divers.

Throw in sunny skies, cooling trade winds and first-rate air connections and you can see why we feel you should head to the "international" corner of the Caribbean on your next vacation.

Contents

Maps

St. Barts

Dreams of Caribbean getaways usually start at the first sign of ice on the windshield of your car. As you stand there scraping it away, you realize there will be many days like this in the months ahead. The thought of a winter respite starts to take hold.

The islands, whether U.S., British or Dutch, offer sunny skies, sandy beaches, active sports, good shops and resort hotels. Unless you have a personal favorite based on past experience, any island will do as long as the airfares and hotel rates are manageable. Only a few islands, such as Jamaica, Puerto Rico and Trinidad, have individual cultures that make them appealing. Add St. Barts to that short list. This is a French island that marches to its own beat and those in the know want to keep it that way.

No splashy advertisement campaigns lure visitors to St. Barts. Instead, people learn about its charm by muted word of mouth. And even that's done subtly, as the people who've vacationed here for years don't want to share their tropical secret. They bemoan the fact that tourism on the island has increased dramatically. Invariably mentioned in the traditional Caribbean guidebooks which touch on every island, and in the literature distributed by the French West Indies Tourist Offices, are the Rockefellers, Rothschilds and Fords, all of whom own villas on St. Barts. It's little wonder that St. Barts is often referred to as "St. Tropez in the Caribbean." These are not big inducements to vacation here, particularly if you've been to St. Tropez lately.

Growth on the island must be kept in perspective. St. Barts today is what St. Tropez was like before Bardot "discovered" it. It's true that new hotels and villa communities have been built, but none is high-rise, none has even 100 rooms, and all are locally owned and managed. All are at the deluxe end of the price spectrum. Although cruise ships now anchor in Gustavia's harbor, there is never more than one a day; the number of arrivals is strictly limited. The island is a duty-free port with wonderful boutiques which, though limited in number, offer a wide variety of merchandise. Still the shops close precisely at noon, not to reopen until 2:30 pm, while the staff enjoys a leisurely lunch. They don't open at all on Sundays.

St. Barts has all the things that have traditionally drawn people to the Caribbean. It has glorious beaches – over 20 of them. The windier part of the island offers great surfing, windsurfing and sailing, while the calmer waters allow for swimming, snorkeling and waterskiing. All these activities – as well as organized scuba trips and day sails – are part of the scene. Additionally, St. Barts has the best restaurants in the Caribbean (French St. Martin will dispute this). French-trained chefs have added Creole,

Thai, Spanish and even cheeseburgers to their traditional French dishes. There are over 50 restaurants to choose from on this small island.

Will you pay a premium to vacation here? Certainly, because you are paying for more than secluded beaches, small posh hotels and great restaurants. You are paying for the special quality of this unique getaway. Only you can decide if it's worth it.

The Island's Name

The name of the island is Saint Barthélemy. It is referred to by traditional islanders as St. Barth, and by more contemporary islanders as St. Bart or St. Barts.

Getting There

By Air

There are no non-stop flights from the U.S., Canada and Europe to St. Barts. Most North American visitors fly directly to Princess Juliana Airport on Sint Maarten, where several commuter lines make the 15-minute flight. Tiny Gustav III Airport can handle only 20-seater "puddle jumpers." The plane heads right at a mountain (called La

Tourmente), clears it by an inch, and then drops steeply to the runway. It's not for the squeamish. The landing strip, the shortest in the Caribbean, ends at the sea.

An alternative is to fly into Puerto Rico or St. Thomas and connect with a commuter plane there. European carriers fly to Guadeloupe, where passengers connect to the commuter lines. If you are staying on the French side of St. Martin, you can take a commuter plane from L'Espérance Airport near Marigot.

Planes can land on St. Barts only in daylight.

The main U.S. carrier to Sint Maarten is **American Airlines** (☎ 800-433-7300). They offer daily flights from Miami or via Puerto Rico. Continental Airlines is also a good choice.

回 TIP

Reserve your commuter airline flight at the same time as you make your long-distance reservation. It is imperative to reconfirm your return flight on these commuter lines.

There are commuter flights virtually every hour from 7 am till 5:30 pm (later in summer). The commuter airlines serving St. Barts are:

Windward Islands Airways	☎ 590-27-61-01
Air St. Barthelemy	☎ 590-27-71-90
Air St. Thomas	☎ 590-27-71-76
Air Guadeloupe	☎ 590-27-61-90

By Boat

Those uncomfortable on small planes have a delightful alternative. Ferries and catamarans connect Sint Maarten/St. Martin with St. Barts daily. The boats are good-sized and modern. It is a lovely ride, taking about one hour from Philipsburg (Dutch) and a half-hour longer from Marigot (French).

The most popular boats are: ***Gustavia Express***, ☎ 590-27-77-24, which has daily crossings leaving from both the Dutch and French sides. The return boat stops in Philipsburg on the way to Marigot. The ***Dauphin II*** (☎ 590-27-84-38) and ***St. Barts Express*** (☎ 590-27-77-24) also make the crossing. The ***White Octopus*** is a catamaran that runs a one-day excursion to St. Barts. It leaves from Bobby's Marina in Philipsburg early in the morning and returns in the afternoon (☎ 599-52-31-70).

The waters are sometimes choppy but never terribly rough.

Entry Requirements

U.S. and Canadian citizens need a valid passport or a birth certificate and a photo I.D. French and EU citizens need a national identity card. All passengers need a return or on-going ticket.

Customs

U.S. Customs

Items purchased in St. Barts fall under the standard $600 duty-free allowance per person. Handicrafts or works of art made on the island are not subject to duty.

Canadian Customs

Canadian citizens can return with $500 Canadian worth of merchandise if they have been out of the country for seven days.

Departure Tax

There is a departure tax of US $12 when flying from Princess Juliana Airport to St. Barts. A $5 tax is charged to those leaving by boat.

Telephones

The area code for St. Barts is 590. If you are calling while on the island, drop the area code and dial only the six-digit phone number.

Getting Around

From the Airport

Most hotels offer a free **airport shuttle service**. Notify them of your flight times and they will meet you there. This is also true for those arriving by boat.

All of the major international **car rental** companies have desks at the airport.

Taxis, which are unmetered, meet every flight. Fix the rate before leaving the airport and keep in mind that fares can quickly add up.

Navigating the Island

> 🔲 **TIP**
>
> There is no public transportation on St. Barts. A few private buses operate, but their routes do not cover the entire island.

Car/Jeep Rentals

We urge you to rent a car for at least part of your stay. This will give you time to explore at your own pace and to return to those spots you enjoy most. Hotels, restaurants and beaches are scattered all over the island and you cannot walk from one to the other easily except in Gustavia. A valid driver's license and major credit card are required.

The most popular rented vehicle is a minimoke, a small, open, jeep-like vehicle that many young locals also drive. It sort of resembles a sideless moving box. The next most popular rental is a jeep. Both operate with stick shifts. A four-wheel-drive vehicle is not a must here.

International rental companies have airport desks. They include:

You can also use the toll-free numbers (look in the Yellow Pages).

Avis	☎ 590-27-71-52
Budget	☎ 590-27-66-30
Hertz	☎ 590-27-71-14
Europcar (National)	☎ 590-27-74-34

 🔲 **TIP**

Make reservations long in advance in high season.

There are many local agencies as well, several of which are associated with hotels. Inquire at the front desk to see if your hotel also rents cars. These include:

Turbe	☎ 590-27-71-42
Gumbs	☎ 590-27-75-32
Chez Beranger	☎ 590-27-89-00
(also rents cycles and scooters)	

Motorbike Rentals

Motorcycles and scooters are very popular on the island. Rates are about $30 per day. Agencies include:

Saint Barts Motorbike	☎ 590-27-67-89
Dennis Dufau	☎ 590-27-54-83
Chez Beranger	☎ 590-27-89-00

Taxis

Taxis are available but not very practical. Privately-owned, they are scarce on Sundays, holidays and after 8 pm. They do not have meters. There are taxi stands. In Gustavia, ☎ 27-66-31 and in St. Jean, ☎ 27-75-81. No tip is expected.

Gas Stations

There are only two gas stations on the island. The larger is near the airport in St. Jean. It closes at 5 pm each night and is closed all day Sunday. You can use a major credit card at the pump here. The smaller station is in Lorient. It keeps the same hours and does not accept credit cards.

Orientation

St. Barts is an eight-square-mile island. It's 4,340 miles from Paris, 1,550 miles from New York and 20 miles from St. Martin. It is home to 6,000 permanent residents, most descended from the original Norman, Breton and Swedish settlers. Newcomers include French citizens who have emigrated to open hotels, restaurants and shops here. Many young French men and women spend a year or two working in the hotels, restaurants, shops and watersports centers.

There are lots of interesting attractions and historical sites on this tiny island. Each is small and can be explored in a short time. The picturesque towns, some with historical interest, can't help but be adjacent to one of the island's 20 beach strips – nothing is more than five minutes from the sea.

One main road covers the northern tier of the island, with smaller roads leading inland to villages and beaches on the less-developed southern shore.

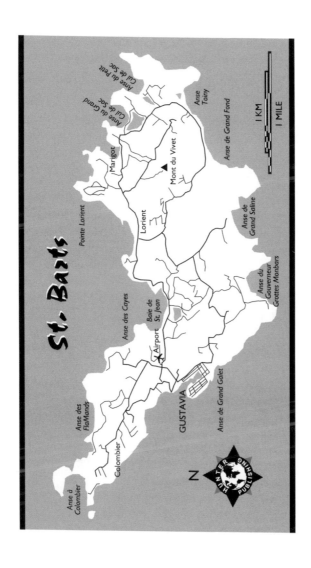

Towns

We'll pinpoint the main towns here, but you'll find more detail about them and the beaches in the *Sunup to Sundown* section.

Gustavia

The capital, on the island's southwestern coast, is a picturesque town laid out around a beautiful harbor, which is usually filled with luxury yachts. It has a mini-mall, boutiques, fine restaurants and bars, historic churches and fort, and even a deluxe hotel. The historical Wall Museum is on La Pointe, the peninsula side of the harbor. There are residences in the higher elevations of the town. Key streets include: **Quai de la Républic** and **Rue de Général de Gaulle** (the two important commercial streets) and **Rue du Centenaire**, the street that connects the two harbor legs.

St. Jean

Located mid-island and on the northern shore, St. Jean is the second largest town and can almost be described as bustling. Tiny Gustav II Airport is here and there are several small shopping centers. St. Jean Beach is the longest and most popular beach on the island, so there are several hotels and restaurants on or near it. Lovely villas sit above the town on nearby hill-sides.

Lorient

Even smaller, Lorient is at the junction of the main road and the road to the island's south shore. It has a school, a mini-market, one of the two gas stations on the island, and two interesting cemeteries. Lorient Beach is the island's best for surfing.

Corossol

On the coast, north of Gustavia, Corossol is a fishing village that has maintained the early traditions. You'll enjoy seeing the Creole houses (*cases*), the older women wearing large white bonnets and modest dress, and visiting the stores that sell the handwoven straw items made here.

Colombier

A tiny residential community on the island's northern fork, Colombier has both traditional and modern homes, lovely gardens and a school. The views from the outskirts of Colombier take in all the offshore islands as well as most of St. Barts. Although it has no beach, you can hike to lovely beach areas from here.

Sights

La Grande Saline

The old salt flats used till the 1970s are now way stations for migrating birds.

Vitet

The highest mountain on St. Barts soars to 900 feet. The island astrologer owns a small inn here.

Geography

The islands of the Lesser Antilles are like tiny blips in a sea of blue. St. Martin and Anguilla are the most northerly islands and St. Barts is 20 miles (32 km) to the south. St. Barts is also much smaller, covering only eight square miles (25 square km). It has an irregular coastline which creates scores of coves and bays, many of which are protected by coral reefs.

St. Barts does not have a single freshwater lake or river. Drinking water is collected in cisterns and saltwater is processed at the local desalinization plant. A rugged mountain range, which includes Vitet, the highest peak, forms the island's spine, creating stunning views.

All roads (paved only in the last 30 years) wind around and over the mountains. Narrow winding roads (also paved) lead from the main road to the coastline.

There is one major road with branches.

Climate

Temperatures are moderated by the trade winds, which cross the island from east to west. Carrying moisture from the Atlantic Ocean (the Atlantic meets the Caribbean off Turtle Island in Grand Cul de Sac), the winds meet resistance at the mountain range. As they rise, they drop their moisture in the form of rain, making the eastern portion of the island green, filled with lush tropical vegetation. This is the windward side (*côte au vent* in French). The western portion of the island gets far less rain and wind. Vegetation on the leeward side (*côte sous le vent)* is sparser, not as colorful, and includes cactus. The vast majority of the flowering plants and trees here have been planted and are tended by residents.

An imaginary line from St. Jean to Gouverneur divides the island into the windward and leeward sides.

Although there is no specific rainy season, St. Barts is in the hurricane belt. In September

1995 Hurricane Luis caused great damage to the vegetation, beaches and buildings.

★ DID YOU KNOW?

Fortunately, a heavy rain a few days after Hurricane Luis washed much of the salt off the vegetation, allowing it to rejuvenate quickly. Although some beaches lost sand, others were enlarged.

 # Flora & Fauna

Plant Life

On the windward (eastern) portion of the island, flowering plants grow wild by roadsides, in ravines and along hiking trails on the hills. You'll see pink, yellow and orange hibiscus, Mexican creepers, frangipani, bougainvillea, flamboyants, white lilies and even orchids. On the leeward (western) side you'll see less vegetation, but locals have done a magnificent job of planting and watering. As you explore the traditional towns of Colombier and Corossol you'll notice the flourishing gardens around the Creole houses.

Animal Life

There is no fresh water on St. Barts, so there are no indigenous animals. Mongoose and iguanas were introduced by settlers. Birds are the most interesting of the wildlife here. The brown pelican is so ubiquitous that it is one of the island's symbols. Watch it glide effortlessly above the sea and then plunge into the water at what seems like 100 mph to scoop up unsuspecting fish. You'll also see black frigate birds with white or red throats, kingfishers, herons, hummingbirds and tiny bananaquits.

In the waters around the island are spiny lobster, dorados, shark, yellowtail snappers, tuna, conch and whelks.

A Brief History

You're going on vacation. There's sea, sand and great food. Who cares about the island's history? Normally we would agree, but in the case of St. Barts, the island is so unusual that you'll definitely be curious. While you may not read this section before you leave home, you surely will after spending a day on the island. We promise to keep it short.

Discovered by Columbus on his second voyage (1493-1496), the island was named for his

younger brother Bartholomew – St. Barthele-
meo. Columbus moved on – with no fresh water
and no people, the island was largely useless to
him. Even the Carib Indians living on nearby
islands stopped here only to fish.

The island was first noted on Spanish maps in 1523.

Although the Pope gave the whole New World
to Spain in 1494, the Spanish did not consider
the tiny islands in this area of any importance
and left them for France and Britain, who both
established colonies on nearby St. Christopher
(now St. Kitts). In 1634, Pierre d'Esnambuc
(sponsored by the French on St. Kitts) landed
on St. Barts and liked it. He set off for France to
gather settlers. He returned to the area with
about 500 people, mostly peasants from Normandy and Brittany. Since the majority of
these people chose to stay on St. Kitts and others on Guadeloupe and Martinique, only 60 or
so arrived on St. Barts in approximately 1648.

The governor of the French colonies,
Longvilliers de Poincy was also a commander in
the Knights of Malta. This order was founded
during the Crusades to aid soldiers and pil-
grims enroute to the Holy Land. As the Spanish
became more prominent in the area, they men-
aced the small French colony. De Poincy sold
St. Barts and the French side of St. Martin to
the Knights, thereby gaining a protective force
while he continued to govern.

Unfortunately, the Knights did not recognize
the threat from the Carib Indians. The Indians
massacred the entire colony, which made it

more difficult to attract new settlers. Yet since it had an excellent harbor and a strategic position surrounded by British possessions, the governor of St. Kitts cajoled 100 hardy Huguenots from Normandy and Brittany to try again.

With no fresh water and little arable land, no plantations were established here and there was no need for slaves. Unlike the majority of islands in the West Indies, there are very few black people living on St. Barts. Those that do live here are descendants of workers from nearby islands recruited to labor in the shipyards.

St. Barts began to prosper because of its harbor. Pirates of all nationalities made the island their headquarters, bringing the treasures they had plundered from Spanish galleons, having their ships repaired and restocked. One well-known cutthroat, Montbars the Exterminator (is that a great name!) made St. Barts his home.

Montbars the Exterminator

As a boy the French-born Montbars had read of the cruelties of the Spanish as they conquered the New World. He vowed revenge and was so successful he earned the name "Exterminator." Montbars was lost at sea during a hurricane and never returned to excavate his loot. Lore has it buried near Anse de Gouverneur or Grande Saline on the south coast. Bring your shovels!

Although prospering, St. Barts was ceded by King Louis XVI to his friend King Gustaf III of Sweden in exchange for free-port rights in Gothenburg. In 1784, the Swedes, who had no other possessions in the New World, became rulers of St. Barts. They took their responsibility seriously. They laid out a grid of streets on both sides of the harbor, renaming the town (then called Carenage) for their King, Gustavia. They carved winding roads through the island, built a town hall, made the island a duty-free port (which it still is today) and constructed three forts. Forts Gustaf, Octave and Karl are still visible today, with Gustaf on the hill in town. Best of all, they did not impose their culture on the islanders, but rather permitted local traditions to continue.

Look for Swedish names on streets.

The island boomed and by 1800 there were over 6,000 residents. Unfortunately, as neighboring islands expanded their port facilities, trade moved north, especially to the Danish Virgin Islands (now U.S.). Many St. Barthians left the island to form a community on St. Thomas. They called it Carenage and it still exists today.

There are about 6,000 residents today as well.

Hurricanes and a huge fire in 1852 decimated Gustavia. It was not rebuilt. In 1967 only 400 people lived in Gustavia.

In 1878, after 92 years, the Swedes sold St. Barts back to France. It remains part of France today, with locals voting for the French President and Prime Minister. It is governed through Guadeloupe, but elects a local mayor and municipal council.

St. Barts remains an anachronism. Older residents cling to the centuries-old traditions of their native Breton, Norman and Swedish ancestors, while the younger are moving rapidly into the world of rock music, Sunday football games and cheeseburgers.

Sunup To Sundown

Since St. Barts' weather is near-perfect year round, you'll spend many of your daylight hours on the beaches, either on a lounge chair working on your tan or enjoying watersports. But the island has over 20 distinct beaches and the coves and bays that house them are on all parts of the island. Virtually every town and village was established near a beach or marina, so you'll be sightseeing as you head to a new beach. Swimming beaches have thick white sand and calm waters. Several have coral reefs that even a beginner can snorkel over, while others are perfect for windsurfing, boardsurfing, spearfishing or shell-collecting.

Beach areas that do not have a hotel are undeveloped. There are no lounge chairs, umbrellas or food. Bring a blanket, find a seagrape tree and bring a picnic lunch. Most of the beach areas are easily accessed by car. You may have a short walk across the dunes from the parking lot. In just a few cases, the hike is a true hike, as in Colombier, and in other cases the access is by boat only. Often, these boat-accessed beaches are popular with local scuba operators.

▣ TIP

All beaches are open to the public, even those that front a hotel. Non-hotel guests can rent watersports gear, eat at the hotel's restaurant, and use the pool for a fee.

Topless bathing is the norm on St. Barts, both on beaches and at poolside. Although nude bathing is officially illegal, nobody pays much attention to it and it is commonplace on isolated beaches on the island's rugged southern shore.

You can play tennis or squash, then go horseback riding or bicycling.

Your beach-hopping and island exploring will depend on what activities you enjoy most, but we'll start where everything starts on St. Barts, in Gustavia, the delightful capital. It is the only place on the island you simply must see. You can easily explore the downtown commercial area on foot.

Gustavia (and Shell Beach)

St. Barts is the only island in the Caribbean that has Sweden as part of its heritage. In this capital (which was named for the Swedish king Gustav) you'll find that the streets have both Swedish and French names. When you shop, you'll sing the praises of good King Gustav, who declared this town a duty-free port, a status it still holds today. Gustavia's beautiful harbor is often dotted with luxury yachts and sailboats tied to its berths. In the distance at the harbor's entrance, you might notice a cruise ship at anchor. The passengers are ferried ashore in dinghies. Don't be alarmed by this onslaught of tourists: The locals, determined not to be over-run by cruise passengers, limit the number of ships.

The town has two legs (on either side of the harbor) and the far side is called La Pointe. It has an old Swedish fort, the newly renovated Wall House Museum and Library, and scores of restaurants, but all the action is on the nearside. It has many restaurants, as well as the shops, historic buildings and an open-air market, Le Ti Marché, which is fun to explore.

There are very few buildings of historic interest left in town because of the damage wrought by a hurricane and then a fire in 1852. The oldest building in town is the **Vieux Clocher**, on Rue du Presbitaire. This bell tower, built in 1799, once sat adjacent to a church that no longer exists. The bell, which rang to mark special events, has been replaced by a clock.

The **Mairie**, now the town hall, was formerly called the Governor's House and used to be the home of Swedish governors. It retains the Swedish architectural style with its green and white façade and stone foundation. It's on Rue Auguste Nyman, which is the continuation of Rue de Roi Oscar II.

You'll want to spend some time at the open-air **Le Ti Marché** (market) that is near the Mairie. Open every day but Sunday, it is part arts and crafts market that sells locally made cosmetics and lotions usually found in upscale department stores stateside and part a fresh produce market. The produce is sold by ladies from Guadeloupe who fly in Tuesdays and return on Thursdays.

Two 19th-century churches, both of which which still hold services, are on the streets just above the harbor. The **Catholic Church** on Rue du Presbitaire (near the old clock tower) was built in 1822. It is similar to the one in Lorient, which was the island's first Catholic church. It has white-washed walls and a lovely garden. Note the bell tower that is both separate and higher than the church, allowing the chimes to be heard everywhere.

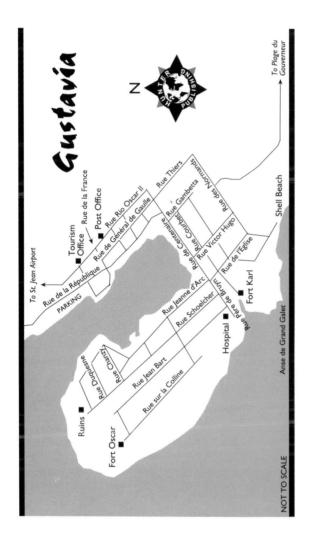

Gustavia

N

HUNTER PUBLISHING

To St. Jean Airport

Tourism Office
Post Office
Rue de la France
Rue Rio Oscar II
Rue de Général de Gaulle
Rue Thiers
Rue Gambetta
Rue des Normands
Rue Cap Centenaire
Rue Courbet
Rue Victor Hugo
Rue de la République
Rue de l'Eglise
PARKING
Rue Jeanne d'Arc
Rue Schoelcher
Rue Pere de Bruny
Fort Karl
Shell Beach
To Plage du Gouverneur
Hospital
Ruins
Rue Duquesne
Rue Charity
Rue Jean Bart
Rue sur la Colline
Fort Oscar
Anse de Grand Galet

NOT TO SCALE

The **Anglican Church** is on Rue de Centenaire, a major street that joins both legs of the
harbor and houses the post office. The church is
starting to show its age and is quite weathered.

★ DID YOU KNOW?

The dark stones on the corners
of the Anglican church were
brought from St. Eustatius
while the stones of the façade
and steps were brought from
France.

The Swedes built three defensive forts around
the harbor. **Fort Oscar** still guards the
entrance at La Pointe, although it is closed to
the public. **Fort Gustav**, at the entrance to
town (near Public Beach) may be visited but
isn't too exciting. **Fort Karl** is only a memory.

The **Municipal Museum & Library** is often
called The Wall House Museum because it is
situated in an old Swedish warehouse of that
name. The building is on Rue Schoelcher at the
farthest point of La Pointe. The front is marked
by cannons and Swedish and French flags. The
inner building was badly damaged by the 1852
fire but, fortunately, the façade remains solid.
Both the museum and library offer a journey
back through time to discover the island's roots.
There are texts, historical engravings and
maps that trace the island from the times of
Columbus to the Knights of Malta, Montbars
the Exterminator and the Swedes. Documents,

watercolors, and portraits abound. It's small but very interesting. Hours are Monday-Friday, 8:30 am to 12:30 pm and 2:30 pm to 6 pm. Saturdays it's open from 9 am to 11 am. Closed Sunday. Small fee.

Two interesting spots are beyond the "downtown" area. The first is **Anse de Grand Calet**, better known as Shell Beach, which is just a five-minute walk from town. Dredging of the harbor in 1960 revealed the shells which continue to wash onto the shore here.

This is not a great swimming beach.

The other point of interest, at Public Beach on the way into town (look for the desalinization plant), is the old **Swedish cemetery**, which has some weathered stones dating from the 18th century. A stone memorial to Swedes who stayed on after the island was returned to France was placed here by Sweden's king when he visited in 1978.

Having exhausted the town's historical sites you have two choices – lunch or shopping. Look for lunch suggestions in the *Dining* chapter.

Saint Jean
(Saint Jean Beach)

Saint Jean Beach, at the heart of the island, is the closest thing to "bustling" that you'll find on St. Barts. There is always something going on in the tiny village, whether it is a plane taking off or landing or people shopping at the three in-town shopping centers, or families swimming, windsurfing or jogging along the island's most popular beach strip.

It's always fun watching the planes, like giant birds, as they swoop over the mountain and immediately drop to the runway. You can't stand at the end of the runway (which stops at the shore), so people head to the top of the mountain which locals have humorously named La Tourmente (The Torment).

Great views of the airport and all of St. Jean.

Two **shopping centers** are directly across the roadway from the terminal. The **Galeries du Commerce Saint Jean** and **La Savane Centre Commercial** have shops that serve both locals and tourists. Tropic video rentals (owned by very nice people), a laundromat and a pharmacy are among the shops, as is a branch of chic clothier Stephanie & Bernard, a sunglass shop, a lingerie shop, and Crazy Discs.

The largest shopping center, **La Villa Creole**, is near the Eden Roc Hotel, which juts out into the bay, effectively breaking the beach into two distinct strips. Shops in this mall sell clothing, handicrafts, English-language newspapers and take-out food. The restaurant in the center serves all day long.

Saint Jean Beach is the most popular beach on the island for local families, flirting teenagers and the young people who work at the shops and hotels. The bay is very long and the wide strip is covered with thick white sand. There are several watersports centers renting snorkel gear, surfboards, windsurfers and other items. They also give lessons. This is a great swimming beach with a natural coral reef. Saint Jean Beach fronts many of the hotels we've detailed and a few others are on the hillsides nearby. There are good restaurants too. The area behind the beach is also residential, with villa communities and individually owned villas overlooking the sea.

Remember that topless bathing is the norm at beaches and pools on the island.

At Saint Jean, the main road continues eastward to Lorient (we will follow it), and there is a branch road leading inland over the mountains to the southern shore.

Lorient (Anse de Lorient)

Lorient, the site of the first French settlement on St. Barts, is a picturesque village that sits on the crossroads of the main road and the road inland to Vitet and the southern coast. The 19th-century **Catholic church** here has been restored. Similar to the one in Gustavia, its bell tower is adjacent to it. Also in town are two **French cemeteries** that are striking because they are so immaculate. The tombs are slightly raised, with crosses marking each headstone. Atop each freshly painted white tomb you'll see lighted red candles and flowers – some fresh and some plastic. On November 1st and 2nd, locals observe All Soul's and All Saint's Day, two traditional Catholic holidays. On those days there are candlelight processions to the cemeteries and the local parish priest leads the marchers in prayer.

Here too you'll find **Le Manoir,** a Norman manor that was built in the early 1600s. It was shipped from France and reconstructed here in 1984 by a French artist. Now a B&B (see *Best Places to Stay*), it has a wonderful garden with a waterfall and lily pond. The "M" line of local fragrances and lotions developed here are sold here as well. A gas station, post office, two mini-markets, several small hotels and an elementary school, where the children are often at play in the yard, make up this town.

Anse de Lorient Beach is extremely long, and, except for Sundays when many local families head there, it is very quiet. While most of the beach has calm waters, the far end has pounding waves that are prime surfing waters, especially in winter. You'll see lots of young people testing the waves.

🔲 TIP

The "Reefer Surf Club," an informal group, meets at Anse de Lorient Beach. They offer surfing advice to beginners and experienced surfers.

Pointe Milou

Pointe Milou does not have a beach but surfers congregate on the rocky shore because the waves are terrific. It is a beautiful area and many of St. Barts' loveliest residences are here.

★ **DID YOU KNOW?**

Rockefellers, Fords, well-known dancers and rock stars have homes above the bay.

Anse Marigot & Grand Cul de Sac Beach

The road starts to climb as it approaches Marigot Bay, which is a popular area for sailing and swimming. At the peak of the hill, you'll see the stunning bay of Grand Cul de Sac. Three of the island's best hotels are on its shores. The Atlantic Ocean meets the Caribbean Sea at Turtle Island here. The bay is quite calm and has coral reefs for snorkelers and three active watersports centers. The center at St. Barth Beach Hotel has a respected windsurf school. You can windsurf, waterski or sail through these waters. The beach is shaded by trees and is the second most popular strip after Saint Jean.

No towns here.

Anse Petit Cul-De-Sac, Anse Toiny & Grand Frond

These coves mark the start of the island's undeveloped and rugged southern shore. The coast is lined by sheer rock cliffs and there is no sand. Boulders near the shore prohibit swimming, but the area does offer beautiful views and the freshest air on the island.

⚠ WARNING

Some intrepid surfers challenge the waves at Toiny, but we don't recommend it.

A few hardy surfers try their skills here too.

At Petit Cul-de-Sac you can see natural caves in the rock walls and nearby you'll spot the local joke called the "**Washing Machine**." Seawater runs into a natural rock pool and swirls around, creating a foam.

★ DID YOU KNOW?

Rocks from Petit Cul-de-Sac were used to build the church in Lorient.

You can follow the footpath from Anse Toiny (near the posh hotel) to Anse Grand Frond. Enroute you'll pass a typical St. Barts cottage called the Cabrette, which was built of stone and withstood even Hurricane Luis. You'll also go by a private chapel built by a family in memory of a loved one. (There are others in Vitet, Saline and Corossol.)

Grande Saline (Anse de Grande Saline)

Enroute to Grande Saline, the road drops to sea level and follows the rugged coast with an occasional wave washing over the road.

回 TIP
Notice the dry rock walls along the Morne Vitet (mountain), which look like the walls on Ireland's Aran Islands.

This part of St. Barts is exciting because it is so undeveloped and wide open. The two cloudy patches you see are the former salt ponds (salines) from which salt was extracted until the 1970s. They look ghostly, especially now that they are enveloped by mangroves with wild vegetation. These salt ponds have become a way station for migrating birds.

Stay left at the crossroads or you will be on your way back to Lorient.

Grande Saline Beach is arguably the most stunning beach on the island. Park in the area provided and walk over the dunes to the pristine beach. As far as the eye can see there is only thick white sand and sparkling blue water.

🔲 TIP

Le Tamarin Restaurant is nearby.

There are no facilities on the beach so bring a blanket, food and water, and enjoy. This beach is so isolated that it is very popular with nude bathers.

Lurin (Anse du Gouverneur)

The area near the town of Lurin, which is residential, resembles areas of rural France, complete with small houses and pretty gardens. The parking lot here is near a private house. Follow the path to the beach, which vies with Grande Saline for the top prize. Shaded by seagrape trees, the sand stretches for over half a mile. The far point, called Grand Pointe, is where the pirate Montbars was supposed to have buried his treasure.

Waves here are great for surfing and swimming.

🔲 TIP

No facilities. Head to nearby Santa Fe Café or bring picnic fixings.

Corossol (Anse de Corossol)

Corossol is a small fishing village in the northwest part of the island. It would be of little interest to visitors but for the fact that it is the most traditional village on St. Barts. It offers a glimpse of life in rural Normandy and Brittany long ago. Many of the residents speak to one another in an old Norman dialect (they speak French too), and some of the older women dress in modest skirts and shoulder-length white bonnets called quicheonettes. Many of them own or work in the handicraft shops that dot the town. The items sold here are woven using the palm of latania trees from nearby Anse des Flamands, which was introduced to the island by a French priest. He taught local women how to weave the palms, which they did while their husbands were at sea. They make Panama hats, wicker baskets, place mats and bags.

Retrace the route to Lurin and back to Saint Jean.

Cases (Traditional Houses)

Corossol also has many traditional St. Barts houses called *cases*. Built to withstand the elements, they sit on a rock base and the lumber is sunk into concrete. The house is low to the ground and all the doors and windows face west (less wind). The red roof is four-sided and bordered by gutters that trap the rain and direct it to cisterns. The house is painted in contrasting pastels. Small, whole families live in one or two rooms.

Hammocks are popular and take up less space than beds. The kitchen is in an adjoining building. This avoids the risk of fire and keeps the house cooler. The house is surrounded by gardens.

The beach at Anse de Corossol is filled with fishing boats and is not one of the best beaches for swimming.

> **◉ TIP**
>
> Visit the Inter-Oceans Museum in Corossol if you like seashells. It has 7,000.

Anse Des Cayes & Anse Des Flamands

These two bays are adjacent to one another on the island's northern coast, but intervening rock cliffs make it necessary to return to the main road and take a branch road to each.

Anse des Cayes, the smaller of the two, is dominated by the deluxe Manapany Cottages. The rest of the cove is residential, with beautiful villas on the hills that encircle the bay. It's hard to believe when you are driving here, but Anse des Cayes is the cove just west of Saint Jean. If you follow the worn path up the hill you'll be overlooking the airport and town. This bay is very popular with surfers because it is unprotected on both sides. Spearfishermen seem to have success at the western end and a few walk-in scuba divers have fun not too far from shore.

⊡ TIP

Chez Ginette, a local watering hole owned by a vivacious islander, is a good spot to sample a refreshing coconut punch.

Anse des Flamands fronts a tiny village of about 300 residents who live in the stunning villas overlooking the beach. Many of the villas are rented out for part of the year. The hills are alive with banana and coconut palms as well as hibiscus, bouganvillea and lilies. The thick white sand strip is so long that the Isle de France Hotel occupies only a tiny portion of it. Shaded by seagrape trees and latania palms, the strip attracts many joggers at dusk.

The waters here are calm and perfect for swimming, snorkeling, and windsurfing.

Paths lead from the beach to the top of the volcano (now extinct) that gave birth to St. Barts long ago. Even more interesting is the rocky winding path that leads to Colombier Beach (about a 25-minute walk – you'll need closed shoes).

You can eat in the beach-side restaurant and use the pool.

If you follow the beach road past Anse des Flamands you'll find a tiny beach, La Petite Anse. There's not much sand but there is great snorkeling. Anse des Flamands is every bit as lovely as Grande Saline and Gouverneur.

Colombier (Colombier Beach)

Unlike its neighbor Corossol, the town of Colombier at the island's northwest tip is quite modern. You'll pass a church, a school and homes as well as many neighborhood shops. As the road enters town, you'll be struck by the awesome views (this part of the island is well above sea level). Its western location assures you that the sunsets are unrivaled, and there are many lookout points in town where you can stop. The best one is near the "Orientation Map," which is carved in stone. It pinpoints all the sights, which include most of St. Barts, the small islands offshore, St. Martin, and, on a really clear day, Anguilla.

Good swimming and snorkeling.

Colombier Beach is stunning and totally pristine, but it is far below the town. To reach it you can follow the trail from the end of town. It's downhill, but remember that you'll have to climb back up. Give yourself 20 minutes going down and at least 10 more (i.e., 30 mins) coming back. You'll find the trail rocky and the vegetation, which includes cactus, quite dry. Since it is easily reached by boat, the beach is filled with sailboats and motorboats.

Hike to Colombier Beach from Anse de Flamands (see entry above).

> 回 **TIP**
>
> Don't forget to bring water as none is available here.

Land-Based Sports Action

The concierge can help you with arrangements.

Tennis & Squash

Courts can be lit for night play. Hotel guests get preference.

Guanahani Hotel, ☎ 27-66-60, 2 tennis courts.

Isle de France Hotel, ☎ 27-61-81. 1 tennis and 1 a/c squash court.

This is St. Barts' only court for squash.

Manapany Cottages, ☎ 27-66-55. 1 tennis court.

St. Barths Beach Hotel, ☎ 27-62-63. 1 tennis court.

Le Flamboyant Tennis Club, ☎ 27-69-82. 2 tennis courts.

Horseback Riding

Ranch des Flamands (Anse des Flamands) has two-hour rides for beginners and experienced riders. Excursions leave at 9 am and 3 pm. ☎ 27-80-72.

Hiking

You can hike on St. Barts but there are only a few marked trails. A beautiful one connects Anse des Flamands and Colombier Beach and a steeper one connects Marigot Bay and Morne Vitet. Check at the tourist office for trail maps and suggestions, or pick up a copy of *The Caribbean: A Walking & Hiking Guide*, by Leonard Adkins.

Bicycle Rentals

St. Barts is quite mountainous. Be prepared for lots of ups and downs. You can bike on the roads and on more rugged terrain. Get details when you rent. All of the places listed here are in Gustavia.

Rent Some Fun (mountain bikes)	☎ 27-70-59
Ounalao	☎ 27-81-27
Ernest Ledee	☎ 27-61-63

Water-Based Sports Action

Snorkeling

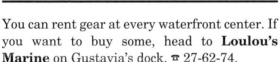

You can rent gear at every waterfront center. If you want to buy some, head to **Loulou's Marine** on Gustavia's dock. ☎ 27-62-74.

Scuba Trips

A variety of scuba trips are organized by certified operators. There are many dive sites near the island, particularly off its western coast. Single- and double-tank dives, night dives, wrecks, deep dives and dives for children are all available. Equipment is provided. Half-day and full-day trips are offered.

West Indies Dives, Gustavia	☎ 27-91-79
St. Barth Diving Ctr. Gustavia Yacht Club Dock	☎ 27-70-34
La Bulle Diving Ctr., Gustavia	☎ 27-62-25
St. Barth Plongée, Gustavia	☎ 27-54-44
Odyssée Caraïbe, La Pointe	☎ 27-55-94

Windsurfing & Sailing

Windsurfing is the most popular watersport here. There are all levels of instruction and the best equipment.

It's a good idea to make plans before your arrival.

Wind Wave Power St. Barths Beach Hotel	☎ 27-62-73
St. Barth Wind School Saint Jean Beach	☎ 27-71-22
Vincent Mistral School Filao Saint Jean Hotel	☎ 22-64-84
Bic Center, Saint Jean	☎ 27-71-22

Parasailing

Wind Wave Power, listed above, offers this sport.

Jet Skiing

Jet Caraïbes, Saint Jean	☎ 27-38-13

Daytrips & Deep-Sea Fishing

These are the two largest watersports centers on St. Barts.

Marine Service Yacht Club Dock, Gustavia	☎ 27-70-34
Ocean Must La Pointe (near Wall House), Gustavia	☎ 27-62-25

Both companies offer half- and full-day sails to secluded bays and uninhabited cays. Snorkel gear is provided. Drinks are included, as is lunch on full-day trips.

Each has crewed charter fishing boats with IGFA-approved equipment. Groups of four or more.

> ### 🔲 TIP
>
> Fishing is best between April and September, but there is fishing year-round. Catches include tuna, bonito, dorado, marlin, wahoo and barracuda.

Captain Jerome Lefort   ☎ 27-62-65
Anse des Cayes.
Big game sport fishing on his Bertram 33.

Yacht Charters & Motorboat Rentals

Nautica FWI, Rue de la République-Wendilia Kronenberg. ☎ 27-56-50; fax 27-56-52. Represents deluxe crewed yachts (one-week minimum).

Poupon Marine, Rue du Roi Oscar. ☎ 27-79-36, fax 27-85-15. Crewed and uncrewed yachts for use by the week or longer.

St. Barth Caraïbes Yachting. ☎ 27-52-48. Motorboats.

Marine Service. ☎ 27-70-34. Motorboats and
sailboats.

Surfboards & Snorkel Gear

Hookipa Surf Shop, Saint Jean (rentals)	☎ 27-71-31
Hookipa Surf Shop, Gustavia (sales)	☎ 27-76-57
West Indian Surf Shop Salinas Road in Saint Jean (rentals and sales)	☎ 27-90-01
Loulou's Marine, Gustavia (sales)	☎ 27-62-74

Waterskiing

St. Barth Caraibes Yachting	☎ 27-52-48
Marine Service	☎ 27-70-34
Ocean Must	☎ 27-62-25
Adventure Trips (Scott Jones)	☎ 27-50-79

Adventure Trips (Scott Jones)   ☎ 27-50-79
Scott offers trips to the island's west coast dive
spots, kayak trips, cliff diving, hiking and
others. Small groups.

Shop Till You Drop

Gustavia

There are two dozen boutiques in downtown Gustavia. Look for them on Rue Général de Gaulle and along Quai de la République, which also has a mall. Shops sell imported fashions from France and Italy for both men and women, jewelry, watches, leather goods, fine cosmetics and lotions, cigars, wine and liquors and local arts and crafts.

> **🔲 TIP**
>
> Gustavia is a duty-free port. This means that the imported sportswear and leather goods are less expensive than they would be in Paris or Milan, but don't expect bargains.

Store Hours

Weekdays, shops open at 9 am (a few open at 8 am). At 12 noon (or 12:30 pm) the doors are locked, the gates are pulled down, and shop owners and salespersons head to lunch. They re-open at 2:30 pm and stay open till 7 pm. On Saturday, stores open from 9 am to 12:30 pm and most do not re-open in the afternoon. Stores are closed on Sundays.

Suggested Boutiques

Most shops accept major credit cards, travelers' checks and U.S. dollars.

Most of the designer boutiques are in **Le Carré d'Or**, a multi-level mall that looks like a mini-version of Los Angeles' Rodeo Drive. It is on the Quai de la République opposite the harbor. **Hermès** and **Cartier** stand at the entrance and you'll find **Polo**, **Versace**, and **Stephane and Bernard**, a local shop that sells imported designer fashions and sportswear. The **Black Swan Boutique** sells bikinis and upscale t-shirts; **Carat** sells jewelry; **Privilege** sells perfumes; and there are any number of interesting shops to rummage through.

Rue de France & Rue Général de Gaulle

Laurant Effel sells fine leather shoes, handbags and belts for both sexes. Highly styled, most are from Paris.

La Comptoir des Antilles sells English language newspapers and magazines.

L'Homme Et La Mer offers fine men's resort wear.

Le Comptoir de Cigare has a selection of the world's best cigars and is the most attractive shop here. Step into the humidor room and select from the Dunhills, Davidoffs, Dominican and Jamaican brands as well as best-sellers from Cuba. They sell humidors and Panama hats as well.

Little Switzerland has shops on every Caribbean island, including St. Barts. An attractive shop selling fine watches, jewelry, crystal and perfumes.

Carat nearby has Christofle pieces as well as Piaget watches, while its neighbor **Kornerupine** sells 18K gold jewelry from Charmet of Paris, Breitling and Jaeger Le Coultre watches and the very hot Ingénieur chrome alarm watch.

La Perla features sexy lingerie, while **Nomades** is an eclectic shop with attractively priced sundresses, pareos, strawbags and t-shirts.

Two great stops for t-shirts and the like are **Outremer** and **Loulou's Marine**. Outremer sells shorts, cotton tote bags and straw items. **Loulou's**, a chandler's shop, sells the white and olive green totebags with their name and logo that are very fashionable here.

Don't forget Le **Ti Marché** open-air market, where you can buy Belou's P (Parfumes et Punches), a line of fragrant oils, shampoos and perfumes created by a local duo. They also market a line of punch drinks. Each of the fragrances is beautifully bottled and named for an island beach. Aromas include amber, vanilla, cinnamon, frangipani and jasmine. Another line of lotions, created at Le Manoir in Lorient and marketed under the name "M," is sold here and at shops nearby.

Le Goût du Vin is another attractive shop selling French wines and champagne (you'll recognize the names).

Pottery is a local handicraft using the traditional method of throwing the clay on the wheel, forming it by hand, then glazing and firing it. Not only are the vases and pots beautifully painted, they are oven-safe. **St. Barts Pottery** has a large selection.

Papagayo, an arts and crafts store, has two shops. They sell silver jewelry, carved wood, hammocks, batiks and pareos. They are open from 9 am to 6:30 pm every day except Sunday.

St. Barts Artists

There are many local artists and sculptors whose work is for sale at their individual galleries and at art galleries around the island. The **Municipal Tourist Office** (at the dock) has a list of artists and galleries. They will tell you which artists are in residence when you are visiting St. Barts and what kind of work they do.

Best Places to Stay

From the air St. Barts resembles a centipede, its irregular coastline creating *anses* (coves), *baies* (bays) and cul-de-sacs isolated from one another by the mountain range that threads through the heart of the island. Virtually all house beach strips and small exceptional hotels are reached by winding paved roads that drop vertically to the sea. Other hotels and most rental villas perch at irregular levels on the green hills that overlook the coast, and there is even a deluxe choice in the capital, Gustavia.

The island has over 40 hotels and a small number of guest houses. While they vary widely in decor and ambience, they share certain characteristics. Hotels are very small (the largest has only 76 rooms). Some of the island's finest stops have fewer than 20 rooms. No more than 600 rooms are available at any one time.

Hurricane Luis not only decimated St. Martin, but swept through St. Barts as well. Although damage here was not as extensive, it did force renovations to rooms and restaurants at several hotels. You will reap the benefits of those facelifts.

Hotels are locally owned and often family managed, and only one hotel is part of an international chain. The owners and staff get to know every guest. They pride themselves on their

European ambience and even deluxe choices have kitchenettes. Some hotels even allow pets. They offer shuttle service to and from the airport, include breakfast in the rate and some offer car rentals.

There are no high-rise hotels, so your accommodation will likely be a private cottage or in a two-story unit. Invariably you'll be two steps from the beach; you'll have a private terrace or patio encircled by grape trees. Many accommodation choices have restaurants, some of which are gourmet, drawing diners from other parts of the island.

St. Barts' deluxe hotels are exceptional. They are elegantly furnished and often have private pools or jacuzzis. They have tennis courts, fitness centers, satellite TV, in-room fax and exercise bikes and serve breakfast on a private terrace. There are few inexpensive stops here, although we have ferreted out a bed & breakfast and several inns.

Because of the paucity of hotel rooms, a popular alternative is to rent a villa – a home away from home. Once again, options and price vary from comfortable one-bedroom retreats to lavish multi-bedroom havens complete with swimming pool and jeep. Villas come with daily maid service. Several villa communities have been built by hotels either on-property or nearby. Villa guests have full hotel privileges. Other villas are individually owned. Rentals are handled by agencies both on the island and abroad.

Things to Consider

Rate Schedules

Hotels have several rates for different times of year. Some have as many as six, but the most common are: December 15-New Year's weekend. The highest rates are in effect during this time period and hotels and villas often require a minimum stay. High season rates are in effect from early January through the end of April and again from November 1 through December 14. Rates are as much as 40% higher than in the off-season.

★ *TIP*

Off-season is quite long, running from May through October. You can save a lot of money by visiting during this time.

Off-Season Travel

One drawback to off-season is that many hotels (restaurants too) close for periods of time, with June, September and October being the most common. There is no routine to these closing times. If your first choice is closed, your second is likely to be open.

Advance Bookings

Make reservations well in advance and make sure you pin down all the things that are important to you, ensuring that all your needs will be met. Hotels, even small ones, have a variety of accommodations.

Alive Price Scale

Rates on the island are very high, reflecting the limited number of rooms. You are paying not just for your room but for the singular quality of the island. While most hotels quote rates in U.S. dollars, some use French francs. Credit cards are readily accepted, although a few smaller stops may require a cash (check) deposit.

Hotels have a wide variety of accommodations. Few fit neatly into our categories of Deluxe, Expensive, Moderate, Inexpensive, and most fit into several categories. The price ranges shown here are designed to give you a heads-up about hotel rates, but always check with the hotel itself.

Rates based on a double room, per night in high season.

Deluxe.	over U.S. $500
Expensive	U.S. $300-500
Moderate	U.S. $200-300
Inexpensive	under U.S. $200

The Best Hotels

Guanahani Hotel

Box 109, Grand Cul de Sac
St. Barts, FWI 97133
☎ (590) 27-66-60; fax (590) 27-70-70
Expensive-Deluxe

Through Leading Hotels of the World, ☎ *800-223-6800.*

Guanahani would be a small luxury resort on any island but St. Barts. Here it is huge. It has 72 rooms, spreads over seven acres, and is fronted by two beaches. A member of The Leading Hotels of the World, Guanahani has "it," but doesn't flaunt it. Everything is understated, using a mélange of pastel shades, tropical woods and Creole furniture to create a relaxed environment.

It is a village of cottages, 40 in all, done in West Indies style, with high pitched roofs and tiled terraces. Accommodations vary, however, in size, decor and, perhaps most importantly, location. There are cottages near the beach, others near the pools, and still more by the tennis courts.

Closed Sept.

🔲 *TIP*

If you like to sleep in, you might not want to be near these facilities, so be sure to check when you make your reservation.

The newest cottages, all suites, sit on a hillside at the edge of the property overlooking a coconut plantation and villa owned by the Rothschild family. These are very modern, with polished wood floors, darker wood furniture, deeper pastels on the walls, a sunken sitting area and handcarved cabinents for the TVs, mini-bar and desk. A curved wall separates the living and sleeping areas. Bathrooms have marble showers (no tubs). Each has a private pool or jacuzzi.

The original cottages are set throughout the property with six facing the beach. Some have double rooms and others have suites. These units are more traditionally furnished than the newer ones, but still offer stocked mini-bars, satellite TVs, air-conditioning and terraces.

Guanahani's main building is a lovely Colonial-style house with a wrap-around terrace. It has a very large lobby that is casually divided into conversation areas. Some guests congregate at the piano, others at the bar or around the comfortable couches.

There are two beaches; two pools, each with lounge chairs and tables; a well-organized watersports center with snorkel gear, windsurfers and jet skis; two floodlit tennis courts; a fitness center; beauty salon; and boutiques.

L'Indigo is an informal restaurant at poolside, while Le Bartolomeo, a gourmet continental choice, is nearby. Each has theme dinners and after-dinner shows several nights a week.

When you pull over at the scenic stop near Marigot Bay and see Guanahani, you realize just how lovely it is.

Isle de France Hotel

Closed Sept.

Box 612, Baie des Flamands
St. Barts, FWI 97098
☎ (590) 27-61-81; fax (590) 27-86-83
Expensive-Deluxe

A personal favorite tucked away in a forest of palm trees on breathtaking Flamands Beach, the Isle de France was built in 1992 and hurricane induced renovations were completed in 1996. The results are stunning – informal yet elegant.

回 **TIP**

The hotel shares the bay with only a few private homes so it is secluded and very private.

The main building, a two-story replica of a Colonial-era plantation house, is a happy blend of old world-style and new facilities. It houses communal sitting areas, a covered terrace, offices, the pool and adjacent restaurant, and a dozen second-story accommodations.

The bulk of the accommodations are in 16 cottages and three beachfront suites. Some cottages are on the beach, but most are across the road in a garden area, where there is an additional pool. All feature antique mahogany furniture, colorful cotton fabrics, local artwork, including some antique prints, double-sink bathrooms and private terraces. All are large and have air-conditioning, ceiling fans and stocked mini-bars. A few garden cottages have kitchenettes.

Isle de France has the best sports facilities on the island, including two spacious pools, tennis courts, an air-conditioned squash court (the only one on St. Barts) and a fitness center. A watersports center is on the beach and a ranch nearby offers horseback riding. You can also jog on the long, quiet beach.

This is the most romantic hotel on the island.

A poolside gazebo houses the La Case de L'Isle restaurant that serves lunch and dinner. Its French-born chef is known for light French dishes. You can order them from room service (24 hours) and dine privately on your terrace. The restaurant is open to the public. Continental breakfast is included in your rate.

Le Toiny
Anse de Toiny
St. Barts, FWI 97133
☎ (590) 27-88-88; fax (590) 27-89-30
Deluxe

Closed Sept. 1 through Oct. 20.

Many would select Le Toiny, a member of the Relais & Chateaux, as St. Bart's most luxurious hideway. Brad Pitt and Gwenyth Paltrow are among those that did. What is most striking about this 12-villa retreat is how determined the owners, architects and interior decorators were to insure guest privacy and comfort. The green peaked rooftops, each on a different level, sit on a secluded promontory overlooking St. Bart's rugged southern coast.

No swimming here, but board surfers take advantage of the rolling waves.

The main building at the head of the driveway houses a small formal lobby decorated with dark woods and pillowed settees. The fashionable Le Gaic restaurant (see *Dining,* below) adjoins the lobby, as does a semi-circular pool and large sun deck. Non-guests who eat lunch at the restaurant may also use this pool. Hotel guests in the one- , two- and three-bedroom suites have private pools and sun decks and the most luxuriously furnished accommodations on St. Barts. They offer polished floors, four-poster beds with mosquito netting, a fax/telephone, satellite TV and VCR, stocked mini-bar, a kitchenette with microwave and icemaker, porcelain vases filled with fresh flowers and a stationery bike. Bathrooms too are exceptional, with walk-in closets, hand-milled soaps and sunken bathtubs.

The ultimate luxury is the continental breakfast served each morning on your private terrace. Fresh tropical fruits and juices, flaky croissants and muffins, yogurt and your favorite beverages on fine china.

Gran Cul de Sac and Saline Beaches are just five minutes away, as are tennis courts. If you have to ask how much it costs, you probably can't afford it. But, if you can, its truly exceptional.

Hotel Manapany Cottages

Open all year.

Box 114, Anse des Cayes
St. Barts, FWI 97133
☎ (590) 27-66-55; fax (590) 27-75-28
Expensive-Deluxe

The steep road to Anse des Cayes, a secluded cove on a rugged coast, is lined by unruly palm trees and thick tropical plants. This "return-to-nature" theme is enhanced by the roar of waves that pound the rocks at the edge of the main house and gourmet restaurant. One would expect a rustic resort, so it is a surprise to find such a luxurious one. Forty-six accommodations are scattered throughout the hotel's 2½ acres. The newest and most luxurious are on the beach, while the majority (20) are in attached red-roofed cottages built on the hillside overlooking the beach and surrounded by trees and gardens.

The dozen "club suites" are decorated in marine, Asian and Caribbean themes, with large marble baths, full kitchens and living/dining areas with glass sliding doors open to the terrace. The hillside cottages are smaller but charmingly decorated as well. Families can ask for an adjoining unit to be converted into a single accommodation (it raises but does not double the cost). Hillside cottages have kitchenettes on their terraces.

Anse des Cayes is a lovely beach which is virtually private. The hotel has placed white umbrella-capped tables and lounge chairs on the beach and around the oval pool. The watersports center has snorkel gear and windsurfers. There is a tennis court and fitness center.

Manapany has an excellent restaurant called Ouanalou. Another good restaurant – New Born – is also on the cove. Hotel guests gather at the piano bar after dinner.

Carl Gustaf Hotel
Rue des Normands, Gustavia
St. Barts, FWI 97133
☎ (590) 27-82-83; fax (590) 27-82-37
Deluxe

The only deluxe hotel located in the capital, the Carl Gustaf is an all-suite gem notched into a hillside at the foot of the harbor. Red-tile roofs top the pale orange buildings, which are enveloped by flowering plants and terraced walkways. There are 14 suites. All, whether one- or two-bedroom, have a private terrace and plunge pool. The living room has whitewashed walls and French doors that open onto the terrace. Decor includes rough marble floors, wicker furniture with colorful nautical and tropical prints. In-room amenities include well-appointed kitchenettes, stocked mini-bars, fax machines, satellite TV and VCR, and a stereo. There is 24-hour room service, a fitness center and a pool. The restaurant (see below) is one of the island's best. You can walk into town to shop or eat and the hotel has shuttle service to nearby beaches.

Closed Sept.

Sofitel Christopher
Box 571, Pointe Milou
St. Barts, FWI 97098
☎ (590) 27-63-63; fax (590) 27-92-92
Expensive

Closed Sept. 1 through Oct. 15

Large by St. Barts standards, the 40-room Christopher spreads along secluded Milou Point on the island's northeast coast. The shoreline is rocky and there is no beach, but you can swim or cool off in the irregularly shaped pool that abuts the shore. Very large, it is encircled and divided into segments by a woodplank sundeck. Small foot bridges head from one area to the other. Comfortable lounge chairs are scattered throughout, many shaded by thatched umbrellas. If you want to enjoy some watersports you can head to Lorient or Cul-du-Sac beaches nearby.

Accommodations in slate-roofed, two-story attached buildings are set in a semi-circle on the nearby hillside, surrounded by a tropical garden.

The green rooftops slope to provide shade for the second-level terraces and the ground-floor patios. Rooms face the sea or gardens. They are large and modern in decor. The carved woods on the bedposts and bureaus are crafted from local trees and the coordinated accessories are floral. Tiled baths have excellent lighting. All rooms are air-conditioned and have stocked mini-bars. You can join the daily aerobics class or work out solo in the fitness center.

Breakfast, which is included in your rate, is served at poolside or in your room. L'Orchidée is the dinner-only French eaterie that draws many islanders for Norwegian salmon blinis or Caribbean sea bass.

Part of the Sofitel chain, the Christopher is one of St. Barts' most attractive stops.

Eden Rock
St. Jean
St. Barts, FWI 97133   *Open all year.*
☎ (590) 27-72-94; fax (590) 27-88-37
Expensive

It's easy to see why Rémy de Haenen, the first man to land a plane on St. Barts and also its first mayor, built Eden Rock, St. Barts' first hotel, on this steep rocky promontory that juts into St. Jean Bay like a giant exclamation point. It is dramatic to look at and it breaks the beach into two strips. Built in the 1950s, it was sorely in need of loving care by the 1990s. Fortunately, a young British couple, Jane and David Matthews, and their two young children purchased the property in 1995. They have made many changes, some necessary and others to upgrade and expand the facilities. They have not changed the hotel's essential character.

The 10 original rooms, six on the rock and four on the beach, have all been renovated. Each room is individually furnished, but they all have terra cotta floors, four-poster beds, print fabrics and lots of British antiques. Some have terraces. They have also burnished the hilltop bar and restaurant, which are first rate. A new pool, bar and restaurant have been completed on the beach and it is possible that new rooms will be added. Breakfast, part of your rate, is served in your room. Because Eden Rock is home to the Matthews family, you'll see water-colors by Jane and her children around.

Hotel Francois Plantation

Closed August 1 through Oct. 3.

Colombier
St. Barts, FWI 97133
☎ (590) 27-78-82; fax (590) 27-61-26
Expensive

In 1987, Francois Beret, a well-known local chef, purchased a manor house on a hilltop on the island's north fork near the village of Colombier. He used the spacious grounds to create an intimate cottage resort that is off-beat both in location and ambience. Although the grounds are large enough to support scores of cottages, the Berets were determined to build a peaceful retreat and therefore built only a dozen, widely spaced and enveloped by lush gardens, where birds sing and where gourmet dining and imbibing are key ingredients.

The main building retains its Colonial architecture and is painted in traditional blue, pink and yellow pastel tones. It has a wrap-around terrace with pillowed wicker chairs and couches where hotel guests and those dining at the restaurant congregrate and sip aperitifs. The inner lobby is quite large, with dark woods and carved mahogany tables and chairs with high

cane backs. There are floral settees throughout
and lots of green plants as well. The Francois
Plantation is known for its first-rate wine cellar, which is open to the public on request.

▣ **TIP**

The gourmet restaurant is re-
viewed in the *Dining* section,
below. Even if you don't stay
here, you can enjoy dinner here
one night.

There are 10 individual cottages and two cottages that can be reconfigured to suit a family
of six. You'll find fresh flowers in each cottage
as well as a queen-sized bed, Caribbean art, colorful fabrics and a stocked mini-bar. Each has a
private terrace (eight face the sea), which has
unusual lounge chairs. Each also offers its own
parking spot.

The sea is a short downhill hike away.

The plantation's pool sits at the top of the resort
overlooking nearby beaches and the coast.

▣ **TIP**

Francois Plantation is in a residential area and is not within
easy walking distance of any
beach or town. A car is a must.

Le Tom Beach
St. Jean Beach
St. Barts, FWI 97133
Closed Sept. ☎ (590) 27-53-13; fax (590) 27-53-15
Expensive-Deluxe

This nondescript building sits roadside and even the small and sparsely furnished lobby is unimpressive. But when you exit onto the beautifully landscaped grounds, you see why this hotel is so popular. The 12 newly renovated rooms are in two-story buildings scattered throughout the property and on the beach itself. Deluxe second-story rooms facing the sea have private terraces and lower-level rooms have patios. Rooms are air-conditioned and also have ceiling fans and mosquito netting around the king-size bed just in case you prefer open windows. Large tiled bathrooms.

Buildings are connected by boardwalk-style plank paths which also lead to the pool, restaurant and beach. Rates include continental breakfast. The restaurant serves breakfast and lunch. Non-guests eating lunch can also use the pool.

Filao Beach Hotel
Closed Sept. 1 through Oct. 17. Box 667, St. Jean Bay
St. Barts, FWI 97009
☎ (590) 27-64-84; fax (590) 27-62-24
Expensive

St. Jean Beach is the hub of action on St. Barts and the Filao Beach Hotel is the center of the hub. Its seaside bar and restaurant are often crowded with beachgoers. Those eating lunch at the restaurant can also use the pool. Wind-surfers, sand volleyball players and joggers keep the beach busy and noisy from early in the morning till dusk. The hotel is an easy stroll to the town, to shops and to restaurants.

A member of the prestigious Relais & Chateaux Association, the hotel has 30 rooms. These are all at ground level, set in a horseshoe shape in a lovely garden. Virtually every type of tree and flower that flourishes in the Caribbean has been nurtured here, and they are all labeled. You'll skirt lily ponds en route to your cottage marked by a colorful ceramic owl.

Deluxe suites face the beach while superior rooms are in the garden just a few steps away. Furnishings are Caribbean-style, not spectacular but well maintained. Breakfast and airport transfers are included in your rate.

You can sit on your terrace and watch the tiny planes land at the airport across the bay.

El Sereno Beach Hotel
Grand Cul de Sac
St. Barts, FWI 97133
☎ (590) 27-64-80; fax (590) 27-75-47
Moderate-Expensive

Closed Sept. 1 through Oct. 15.

El Sereno is one of St. Barts' most popular hotels. Its appeal is obvious. It has a fabulous location on the bay side of Grand Cul de Sac, and its sandy beach is both long and wide. There's also an offshore coral reef that even beginner snorkelers can enjoy.

It has recently refurbished 19 of its garden bungalows and has added five new beachfront junior suites to the nine previously built. Walls are painted in pastel tones and the furnishings are contemporary with red checks and florals on the beds, comfortable armchairs and curtains. Suites have terraces facing the sea while bungalows have flower-filled patios. Hammocks sway beneath the shady palm trees. All accommodations are air-conditioned, have stocked mini-bars, color TVs and VCRs and large bathrooms.

What makes El Sereno stand out is that in spite of its being "serene," as it's name suggests, it just bursts with activity day and night. It has a large freshwater pool and the sundeck and beach have lounge chairs. Nearby, the hotel's watersports center has windsurfers, jet skis, Hobie cats, canoes and snorkel gear. It can arrange for scuba diving trips. You can play tennis or work on your pecs in the well-equipped fitness center. The rolling waves take the place of work-out videos. Continental breakfast is included.

The West Indies Café, roof-covered but open-sided, sits at poolside and offers market fresh daily menus for lunch and dinner and a lively late-night revue as well.

El Sereno has built a small villa community nearby (see below), but it also has a special villa (called Seba) on property. Seba has two bedrooms, a large living/dining area and a fully equipped kitchen. The terrace faces Marigot Bay. Guests have full hotel privileges.

St. Barth Beach Hotel
Box 580, Grand Cul de Sac
St. Barts, FWI 97098
☎ (590) 27-60-70; fax (590) 27-75-57
Moderate

If you need elegant furnishings and a host of amenities to enjoy your vacation, then the St. Barth Beach Hotel is not the place for you. This is one of the island's older hotels and it is comfortable rather than elegant. It does, however, offer many amenities that more expensive hotels have.

It has a wonderful location on Grand Cul de Sac with a wide sandy beach on the sheltered side of the cove. It has the best watersports center on the island for windsurfers, with a school for beginners and advanced surfers. They also rent surfboards, Hobie cats, waterskis, jet skis and sunning mats. Non-guests can rent equipment as well (the center does not belong to the hotel). Le Rivage (see *Dining*, below) is an excellent restaurant. There is a large pool, a sundeck and a tennis court.

There are 16 attached bungalows as you enter the hotel grounds. Just a few steps from the beach and pool, they have kitchenettes, air-conditioned bedrooms and ceilings fans elsewhere. Each has a small terrace and barbecue. Furnishings are well worn but comfortable. The majority of the rooms (36) are in the main building on the beach. Air-conditioned, they have TVs, VCRs and small terraces. This is a very good choice for those with young children. You can easily walk or jog to El Sereno Hotel nearby.

🔲 TIP

The hotel offers several special package deals. Inquire before making your reservation.

St. Barth Beach Hotel has a villa community, Residence Saint Barth on Petit Cul-de-Sac near the luxurious Toiny Hotel.

Village St. Jean

Open year-round.

Box 623, St. Jean
St. Barts, FWI 97098
☎ (590) 27-61-39; fax (590) 27-77-96
Inexpensive-Moderate/Expensive

Pioneers when they built Village St. Jean 17 years ago, the Charneau family, originally from Guadeloupe, continues to oversee the resort today. Père Charneau wanted a village effect so he constructed cottages in a semi-circle across this rolling hill that overlooks St. Jean Beach and the airport. Stone paths that crisscross the grounds connect the cottages to the main house, restaurant and pool.

There are some rooms in the main building, which is marked by a small bustling lobby where Catherine Charneau holds court. She grew up here and her island tips are invaluable.

These rooms are the least expensive accommodations. They have twin beds, small sitting areas and terraces with kitchenette facilities that face the beach.

The newly refurbished cottages have one or two bedrooms with king-sized beds, teak and cane furniture, floral bedspreads and blue tiled baths. Private garden patios or terraces front each lodging. Each has a fully equipped open-air kitchen area, lounge chairs and hammocks. There are 25 rooms in all.

The grounds are beautifully landscaped and the large sundeck that surrounds the pool has a waterfalll and jacuzzi. It is the meeting point for guests. Le Patio, the on-property restaurant, serves breakfast and has take-out service should you prefer to dine on your terrace. A great location, only a few minute's walk from the beach and La Villa Creole Shopping Center, makes this an excellent choice.

Le Patio serves Italian food. It's closed Wednesdays.

Tropical Hotel
St. Jean Bay
St. Barts, FWI 97133
☎ (590) 27-64-87; fax (590) 27-81-74
Moderate-Expensive

Closed May 31-July 15.

Small and intimate, more like a country inn than a hotel, the Tropical has a terrific location on a hillside that overlooks St. Jean Bay. It is adjacent to the Village St. Jean Hotel. A five-minute stroll (downhill) brings you to the beach, several inexpensive restaurants, and a shopping mall, La Villa Creole.

The 20 cottages, built like typical *cases*, are set around a central courtyard. Some face the bay and others the flower-filled garden. Many have private terraces. They've been redecorated with whitewashed walls, air conditioners, TV (no satellite) and white headboards that feature carved pineapples. Comfortable but not elegant. Continental breakfast (included) is served in the garden lounge and there is a small bar serving light food at the pool and sundeck. In high season, a local band plays at happy hour. Children under four stay free.

Nice stop but is overpriced when compared to other spots.

Hotel Yuana
Anse des Cayes
St. Barts, FWI 97133
☎ (590) 27-80-84; fax (590) 27-78-45
Moderate

Open all year.

The Yuana is not an exciting stop when compared to other hotels on the island, but it is an excellent choice for families not needing resort amenities. Hidden from view by flowering vines and luxuriant greenery, the gingerbread-trimmed cottages with turquoise roofs and terra cotta walls are on a hill high above lovely Anse des Cayes Beach. Family-owned, the property is beautifully maintained and each of the sparkling 12 units is a suite with a king- or queen-sized bed and a sofa that can sleep two children. The blue and coral tropical rattan and wicker furniture is user friendly and each air-conditioned room has a TV, VCR and tiled bathroom. There is a fully equipped kitchenette so you can prepare your own meals (although you can also order breakfast from the hotel). You will enjoy the view from your private terrace and you can swim in the good-sized pool.

◙ TIP

Becuase of its out-of-the-way location, a car is a must here at Hotel Yuana.

Hotel Emeraude Plage
Baie de Saint Jean
St. Barts, FWI 97133
☎ (590) 27-64-78; fax (590) 27-83-08
Moderate

Open all year.

Emeraude Plage is an informal hotel that is well run and well maintained, and so it has a loyal repeat following. Guests congregate in the comfortable lobby, which is furnished with bamboo couches and chairs covered in bold Native American patterned prints.

◙ TIP

A focal point here is the used-book library filled with books on many subjects and in many languages. Guests borrow from and replenish the supply.

The hotel is on St. Jean Beach, the island's most popular sand strip, and guests use the water-sports centers and many restaurants on the beach (Emeraude Plage has no private facilities, not even a pool).

Lodging consists of 24 comfortable and spacious cottages, three suites (two-bedroom) and one deluxe villa (two-bedroom/two-bath). Scattered through the property, they are shaded by sea-grape trees, which also provide a measure of privacy from beach passersby and from one cottage to the other. Cottages are whitewashed with peaked beamed ceilings and colorful fabrics. Air-conditioned, each has an equipped kitchenette on its terrace and daily maid service. A good choice for self-starters.

Hostellerie des 3 Forces

Closed July.

Vitet
St. Barts, FWI 97133
☎ (590) 27-61-25; fax (590) 27-81-38
Inexpensive

Whether you are an Aquarian or a Leo, you will enjoy this tiny (eight-room) inn owned by a St. Barts character, Hubert Delamotte. He is the island astrologer and while we don't know first-hand, lore has it that he is very fluent and very funny in French, English and German. The cottages are on a hilltop in a secluded part of the island. Each is decorated in West Indies style, and according to astrological color schemes. Each has air-conditioning and a terrace with a view of the ocean. There are four-poster beds and furnishings specific to the astrological sign of that room. The restaurant offers French cuisine with many vegetarian dishes. There is a small pool. Stop in for a drink at the bar as you explore the island.

Manoir de Saint Barthelemy

Lorient
St. Barts, FWI 97133   *Open all year.*
☎ (590) 27-79-27; fax (590) 27-65-75
Inexpensive

Looking for something a little different? How about a bed and breakfast St. Barts style? A 17th-century Norman country house is the hub of this colony started by French artists. Rather than a room in someone's home and a bathroom down the hall, you'll have your own cottage (with one to three bedrooms), king-sized beds, kitchenette, ceiling fans and full baths. The grounds are lovely, filled with mango and papaya trees, hammocks and a small waterfall that replenishes a pond stocked with tropical fish and plants. You can easily walk to the beach. There is a mini-mart in town but no restaurant nearby. Breakfast is served in your room or in the main house.

Sea Horse

Anse de Marigot
St. Barts, FWI 97133   *Open all year.*
☎ (590) 27-75-36; fax (590) 27-85-33
Inexpensive-Moderate

Small and private with savvy owners, Sea Horse has 10 bungalows and one villa. All are air-conditioned, have fully equipped kitchen areas and terraces that overlook Marigot Bay and Marigot Bay Restaurant (see *Dining*, below). The hotel is up a steep hill from the roadway, which makes for lovely views.

Built in 1988 and redecorated in 1994, the villa has two bedrooms and is near the pool. The one-bedroom bungalows are set in an attractive garden. Small and basic, they have tiled floors, light formica and foam-covered couches and chairs.

You'll be served a welcome drink at poolside and there are BBQ pits should you care to use them. There is a used book exchange in the lobby. Breakfast is the only available meal, but the Marigot Bay Restaurant is across the road.

回 TIP

The owners, who go out of their way to be helpful, offer shuttle service to and from the airport, but a rental car is still a must.

Marigot Bay Club

Marigot

Open all year.

St. Barts, FWI 97133

☎ (590) 27-75-45; fax (590) 27-90-04

Moderate

Best known for its excellent restaurant that sits above Marigot Beach, the club has six small rooms in one building across the roadway. Each has one air-conditioned bedroom, a kitchenette, small sitting area and terrace. Adequate, but uninteresting. There is daily maid service but no other facilities. A car is a must.

Les Mouettes

Lorient Beach
St. Barts, FWI 97133
☎ (590) 27-71-91; fax (590) 27-68-19
Inexpensive

Open all year.

This is as basic as it gets on St. Barts – with the exception of Lorient Beach, the best surfing beach on the island. There is a mini-mart across the road should you want to cook. The seven air-conditioned rooms are furnished in motel style with two beds, a dresser and table that is both a desk and dining area. The bathroom is sans tub. A plus is the kitchenette with stove, refrigerator and utensils. A small terrace faces the beach. There is daily maid service.

MC/Visa accepted only reluctantly.

Les Islets Fleuris

Hauts de Lorient
St. Barts, FWI 97133
☎ (590) 27-64-22; fax (590) 27-69-72
Inexpensive

Open all year.

Another simple choice for people who don't intend to spend much time indoors, Les Islets Fleuris is in the hills above Lorient. Your accommodation will be a small cottage with a comfortable bed enclosed by mosquito netting, a bathroom with only a shower, a fully equipped kitchenette and a comfortable terrace facing the garden or the sea. One of the cottages offers a living room, and there are a total of six studios and one suite. There is a small pool on the property. A small charge is made for breakfast and for a TV/VCR.

Villa Rentals

There are a number of reasons villa rentals are a very popular alternative on St. Barts. Many celebrity visitors opt for the privacy and serenity offered by villas, while families with children enjoy the home-away-from-home feeling, with extra space, and without the headaches. A very practical reason why villas are so popular is because there are only 600 or so rooms available on St. Barts at any one time, and it can be difficult to get space during holidays and in the high season. And finally, but certainly not insignificantly, is the idea that you can save quite a bit of money, especially if you have a large family or can share a spacious villa with friends or family members.

Keep in mind that villas run the gamut from a one-bedroom on the beach to a five-bedroom pad with a private pool and everything in between. Rental agencies will send you a complete listing of what is available.

Hotel Villa Communities

Two hotels have built "villa" communities near their properties. These are very different from private villas. They are hotel-type accommodations without major amenities, but they do offer full use of hotel facilities.

Les Résidences Saint Barth are five minutes from the hotel by car. There are 20 vil-

las (one- to three-bedroom), seven of which
have private pools. All have private terraces, fully equipped kitchens and modern
baths. They are in attached two-story buildings with ocean views. Contact them at
Petit Cul-de-Sac, St. Barts, FWI 97098.
☎ 27-85-93; fax 27-77-59.

*Owned by St.
Barth Beach
Hotel.*

El Sereno Villas are just off the main road
at the turnoff to Grand Cul de Sac and two
minutes from the hotel by car. There are
nine one-bedroom villas in air-conditioned
units with full kitchens. Contact El Sereno
Hotel, Grand Cul de Sac, St. Barts, FWI
97133. ☎ 27-64-80; fax 27-75-47.

Villa rental rates vary according to the available facilities, the season, and the number of
bedrooms you need. Generally speaking, you
should figure two people to a bedroom. For villa
rentals, the high season runs from December 15
through April 15. There is normally a one-week
minimum stay required, and a 10-day minimum between Christmas and New Year's. Off-
season rates are reduced by as much as 40%.

Rental Agencies

The largest rental agency on St. Barts is **Si-
barth Villas**. Their office is on Rue Général
de Gaulle in Gustavia. ☎ 27-62-38; fax 27-
60-52. They are represented by WIMCO
(West Indies Management Co.). In the U.S.,
☎ 800-932-3222 or fax 401-847-6290.

Another well-known firm is **Villas of Distinction** in Armonk, New York. ☎ 800-289-0900 or fax 914-273-3387.

Primbarth Real Estate is the rental agency for the stunning villas in Les Jardins de St. Jean, a community on the hillside above the town. ☎ 27-70-19; fax 27-84-40.

Also try **Ici Et La** on Quai de la Républic, Gustavia. ☎ 27-78-78 or fax 27-78-28.

Best Places to Eat

St. Barts, a very small island, is home to over 50 independent restaurants, one for every one hundred residents. Several would stand out in Paris or New York. These are either owned by European-trained local chefs, or make use of hired master chefs from France to oversee their kitchens. A few of the exceptional restaurants are in hotels. There are bistros, brasseries, rotisseries and cafés as well. Visiting gourmets can be adventurous both in cuisine and ambience.

Most menus feature French cuisine using oysters flown in from Brittany, pâtés and cheeses from Provence and wines from other parts of the country. Meats and fresh produce are imported from the U.S., while fish and shellfish are often from local waters. Preparation varies from traditional to nouvelle and there are some

Creole dishes too. Those featuring the local spiny lobster (langouste) lead the list. Continental restaurants have eclectic menus that roam the globe, blending tapas from Spain with pastas from Italy and lots of Southeast Asian specialties.

> ◨ **TIP**
>
> Because so many items are imported, you'll find the restaurants pricey, but even the most expensive eateries will have a good value prix-fixe menu. By selecting carefully, you can keep your costs down.

Restaurants are informal and relaxed. Their ambience comes from a stunning location at seaside or atop a hill that overlooks the coast. You can dine on a tree-filled patio, in a flowered garden or on a quaint capital street. Music, whether live or on disc, is more often Mozart than Marley. Good food, fine wines and lovely settings all combine to slow your inner clock.

Dining Hours

Restaurants, even those in hotels, serve lunch from noon until 3 pm, then close until 6 or 7 pm, when most re-open to serve dinner till 10 or 11 pm. An interesting dining phenomenon here are the gourmet beachside restaurants that serve lunch only. We will detail them for you.

Most gourmet restaurants serve only dinner (we will detail many of those as well). European visitors and locals enjoy long leisurely lunches, making it the day's main meal. North American visitors crowd the better restaurants at night. Never fear! You won't go hungry. There are cafés and small restaurants that stay open from early morning till late at night.

Dining Savvy

- ⊚ Restaurants are small. Reservations are a must in-season and a good idea year-round.

- ⊚ Restaurants add a 15% service charge to your bill so you should not tip an additional 15%. It is common to leave a small additional tip if the service was good.

- ⊚ Many of the better restaurants close for a time in the off-season. Closings vary. If your first choice is closed, you'll still have many options.

- ⊚ Most restaurants accept major credit cards, but a few small local spots do not. These are noted in the text. You can also pay in U.S. dollars, but you will get change in French francs.

- ⊚ Casual chic attire is the norm at lunch and dinner. Shorts and bathing suits are okay at beachside or poolside spots. Jackets are rare; ties are unheard of.

- ⊚ Virtually every menu has a vegetarian dish or two.

Alive Price Scale

Designed to give you some idea of prices, the Alive Scale is based on a three-course dinner for one person without drinks, service or sales tax.

Very Expensive . . . . over $65

Expensive $50-65

Moderate $35-50

Inexpensive . . . . under $35

Lunch prices are lower.

Exceptional Dining Spots

François Plantation
Colombier
☎ 27-78-82
Very Expensive
Dinner Only

Closed August 1 through October 15 and Sundays.

Typically, where we find an exceptional hotel there is a fine restaurant on the premises. Here we find an exceptional restaurant that has a hotel built around it. Owner François Beret made his name on St. Barts as the chef at several gourmet restaurants. In 1984 the Berets decided to open a place of their own and selected a Colonial manor house near Colombier. They built 12 typical St. Barts cottages for guests, planted wonderful gardens and renovated the manor house to serve as the hotel lobby, a breakfast nook and a cocktail/tea lounge. The wrap-around terrace has comfortable wicker chairs and couches where diners wait for tables or enjoy after-dinner drinks.

The restaurant, reached via a flower-filled arborway, looks like a formal living room with carved mahogany tables, highbacked chairs and white latticed place mats. Mr. Beret is no longer the primary chef, but he continues to work with the French chefs he hires to prepare dishes in his preferred nouvelle style.

Start with goat cheese ravioli, mussel soup or foie gras, then continue with breast of duck with mangoes and ginger, sweet and sour rack of lamb or scallops sautéed and rolled in pan-fried rice.

★ DID YOU KNOW?

A specialty of the restaurant is *coutancie*, beef from cattle that are fed beer every day and have their bodies rubbed down twice daily. The beef is incredibly soft.

One of the best desserts is a chocolate tart with vanilla ice cream. Francois Plantation is arguably St. Barts' finest restaurant.

Le Gaic
Toiny (Toiny Hotel)
☎ 27-88-88
Very Expensive
Lunch and Dinner, Buffet lunch on Sunday.
It's difficult to imagine a formal dining room that is adjacent to a swimming pool and sundeck and where the background "music" is the sound of waves crashing into the shore. But Le Gaic is just that and it would be right at home if it were suddenly transported to New York or Paris. The tables are covered with rich blue fabric, the fine china is white with matching blue trim and the stemware is blue as well. High-back navy blue chairs are placed at each table. The menu is classic French, but a few Creole touches and ingredients creep in.

Closed Tuesday off-season and from September 1 through October 20.

Le Gaic's terrace is partly open-air and partly roof-covered and fan-cooled. At lunch, many guests select the informal open-air tables and take a swim after lunch. There is a prix-fixe lunch and such à la carte items as chilled mango soup, shrimp salad with spicy yogurt dressing, scrambled eggs or smoked sliced chicken with gingered grilled vegetables.

Dinner is a lot more formal, both in ambience (dim lights, music) and menu. Smoked salmon with vegetable blinis, conch ravioli with garlic sauce or duck carpaccio are great openers. Main courses include rack of lamb in a clay shell with sweet potatoes, hen stuffed with wild mushrooms, and shrimp wrapped and fried with a peppered red wine sauce.

You can linger after dinner and enjoy aperitifs on the sundeck, now moon-lit and star-covered. Le Gaic vies with Francois Plantation as St. Barts' finest. It's a special spot for a special occasion.

Chez Maya

Public Beach

☎ 27-75-73

Closed June & September

Moderate-Expensive

Dinner only; closed Sundays

Maya's makes the point that "it's the food, stupid." If the food is good enough, people will come. And they do – in bunches – both locals and celebrities and ordinary visitors like us who've read about this innovative restaurant in a spate of articles in both travel and food magazines.

Randy and Maya Gurley opened their roof-covered, open-terrace eaterie on Public Beach near Gustavia, not the best location on St. Barts. They installed white formica tables and multi-colored director's chairs and lots of flowers. Then they let the innovative, delicious dishes speak for themselves. Maya, the chef, was born on Martinique, where she mastered French cooking early on. The heart of the menu is French, as are the wines. But over the years Maya has expanded her horizons to include

Creole, as well as Thai, Vietnamese and other Oriental dishes. The menu, which changes nightly, is always a blend of cuisines. Each night Maya and her staff prepare five appetizers, five entrées and five desserts.

🔲 TIP

Decisions are hard to make, but if you have a group you can order all selections and sample a bit of each.

Favorites include tomato and mango salad, salmon teriyaki, duck à l'orange, squash fritters and curried sweet potato salad. Thick chocolate cake is a good dessert choice.

Carl Gustaf Restaurant

Rue des Normands (Carl Gustaf Hotel)
☎ 27-82-83
Very Expensive

Closed Sept. and for lunch during off-season.

Carl Gustaf is a small luxury resort notched into a hillside with a panoramic view of the capital and its harbor.

★ DID YOU KNOW?

Because of the limited space available, the architects placed the tiny lobby, gourmet restaurant, pool and piano bar together on a large terrace at the hotel's highest level. It doesn't sound great but it works.

Guests eat lunch on the open-air terrace or the adjacent tables that are roof-covered and fan-cooled. The view is constantly changing as yachts, sailboats and ferries glide into berths at the dock. The informal menu includes lobster salad, shrimp dishes, creamed soups and grilled meats. Many diners take a dip in the pool.

By nightfall, the staff has set the tables with starched tablecloths, napkins, fine china and stemware. The view is the fabulous sunset and then a star-filled sky. The pianist arrives, the bar is crowded and the staff is immaculately attired.

The French menu has a few Creole touches. You can select your wine from their ample wine cellar. Good starters include the circle of prawns and avocados, Andalucian gazpacho or lobster spring rolls. Follow with prawn risotto, roasted salmon with vanilla sauce and sweet potato, fricassée of shellfish with pasta, lamb with crêpes and veal cutlets Provençal. Fruit tarts and crème brûlée are good desserts. This is one of the finest restaurants on St. Barts.

Gustavia

Closed Sundays off-season, as well as during early May and late October.

Le Sapotillier
Rue du Centenaire
☎ 27-60-28
Expensive
Dinner only

Whether you reserve an indoor table or one in the garden under a namesake sapotilla tree, you'll enjoy the experience. Look for the typical St. Barts *case* (Creole for cottage) on the street that connects the two legs of Gustavia Harbor. It looks like a private home and the service is so unrushed that it is easy to forget you are in a restaurant. Brick walls, starched white linen cloths, gaily painted wooden chairs and color-filled Creole paintings add to your pleasure. Those seated in the garden will enjoy the cooling trade winds and starry skies.

While the decor is quite simple, the menu is anything but. Serving traditional Provencal food, Le Sapotillier is best known for its seafood dishes, particularly those using sea bass and huge shrimp. Frogs' legs fricassee or lasagne d'escargots may not sound like something Grandma made, but are actually delicious, as is the roasted Irish salmon. Those who prefer meat will enjoy the filet of beef with morels or the classic duck with peaches. There are prix-fixe French and Creole menus nightly.

🔲 TIP

Save some room for the soft apple cake with ice cream. If it tastes surprisingly like strudel, it may be because both the owner and the chef are Austrian.

La Mandala

Rue Thiers

☎ 27-96-96

Expensive

Lunch and dinner; Sunday brunch

Location! Location! Location! La Mandala has the best location in Gustavia – on a hill overlooking the town and harbor. Opened in late 1995, just missing Hurricane Luis, the Mandala is a Buddhist symbol of harmony. The square within a circle symbol is mirrored in the restaurant by the square table for 10 placed above a glassed circular pool. It's striking!

The sloped beamed ceiling covers the dining terrace, which has tile floors, pillowed barrel chairs and widely spaced tables in a variety of shapes. The room's open feeling is enhanced by the music of the wind chimes.

The crowd arrives at 5 pm, vying for one of the open-air tables or a place at the bar where they enjoy the fabulous tapas and the sunsets. The menu is eclectic and changes daily, mixing French, Creole and Asian dishes. Typically, you'll find salmon carpaccio, tuna sashimi, spicy Thai rolls, grilled lobster, filet of beef and chicken soup, of all things. There is a prix-fixe menu. Lunch features salads and pastas.

La Mandala is near the Carl Gustaf Hotel and other restaurants.

Au Port

Rue du Centenaire
☎ 27-62-36
Expensive

One of the oldest restaurants on the island and among its most formal, Au Port continues to please. In a private house on the Rue du Centenaire, the restaurant is on a roof-covered open porch on the second floor. Subdued indirect lighting bathes the carved mahogany chairs and pink-covered tables in a romantic hue. There are fresh flowers and green plants everywhere.

Owner/Chef Alain Bunel is a master of French/Creole dishes and there is a Creole prix-fixe menu nightly. Conch and lobster sausages, crab and conch ravioli and the lobster casserole are staples. This is a perfect spot to sample stewed goat with curry sauce and bananas. Less adventurous? Stick to the chicken stuffed with foie gras and morel mushrooms or the filet of sole with champagne sauce. Save room for the chocolate mousse cake. Exceptional wine list.

The Wall House

Rue Schoelcher, La Pointe
☎ 27-71-83
Expensive

A neighbor of the museum and library of the same name, the Wall House could easily be called the "White House" as it is glistening white from its wicker furniture to its tile floors, its walls and the cloths that cover tables on a covered terrace facing the harbor. Some tables are on an outer terrace. Color is provided by tall green plants and fresh flowers strategically placed to create dining areas. The menu is French and Creole. Start with gravlax with dill sauce, gazpacho or eggplant mousse. Grilled prawns marinated in whiskey, shark in lobster sauce or beef with pepper sauce are very popular. There are two prix-fixe menus each night as well as a special lobster menu. Lunch finds grilled fish and meats, toasted sandwiches and assorted salads. This is a good choice for both lunch and dinner.

L'Entrepont/L'Escale

Closed Sunday off-season.

Rue Jeanne d'Arc, La Pointe
☎ 27-90-60/27-81-06
Moderate
Lunch and dinner

St. Barts' Italian contingent has found a niche on La Pointe, the far side of Gustavia's harbor. Two excellent Italian choices are just blocks apart.

Moderate.

L'Entrepont is the more formal of the two. Its cloth-covered tables are set in a garden shaded by coconut palm trees and umbrellas. You can see the water from most tables and there is always a cooling breeze. Start with a Caprese salad, eggplant carpaccio or mussels au gratin. There are lots of pastas with a variety of sauces. Veal Milanese or pizzaiola and osso bucco are delicious with Northern Italian seasoning. Many people come for the pizzas (especially at lunch) and there are lots of salads as well.

L'Escale is more like a pizzeria. It draws people to its bar before and after dinner. On a terrace facing the harbor, it has wicker chairs, glass-topped tables and placemats. Many young locals come here after finishing work to relax at the bar and enjoy the pizzas baked in a wood-burning oven. The specialty of the house, surprisingly, is an exceptional steak tartare. Also on the menu are lasagne, ravioli, pastas and veal dishes. The staff has worked here for many years and they are well-liked by St. Barthians.

Open daily from 11 am to midnight. Moderate.

Chez Domi

Rue du Général de Gaulle
☎ 29-84-11
Moderate
Lunch and dinner

Open all year.

Chez Domi would look right at home in St. Thomas or Tortola. It is a typical Caribbean Creole restaurant with one air-conditioned dining room and one roof-covered terrace cooled by ceiling fans. Both have deep blue tablecloths and light wood tables and chairs. Since Creole cooking relies heavily on the freshest catches and produce available, you never know what will be on the menu. If they are on offer, try stuffed crabs or garlicky baked snails for openers and West Indies fish stew in Creole sauce or crayfish with rum sauce for an entrée. Pastas are homemade. The food is delicious and the service is unhurried. A local handicraft shop is part of the restaurant.

Le Vietnam
Rue du Roi Oscar II

Open all year.

☎ 27-81-37

Moderate-Inexpensive

Right in the heart of Gustavia, Le Vietnam, which serves both lunch and dinner, is true to its name and the nationality of its owners. It serves Vietnamese food but its extensive menu also offers Thai and Chinese dishes. The air-conditioned dining room is very attractive, with white starched tablecloths covered by thick glass, hanging Chinese lanterns, decorative red fans and large fish tanks. These fish are for decoration only, but there are many fish dishes on the menu. You'll enjoy the mahi mahi with hot and sour sauce and the crispy shrimp fritters. The soup Hanoienne with shrimp or pork is enough for an entire lunch, but hearty eaters can follow it with Vietnamese egg rolls, duck with pineapple or sweet and sour pork. You can also eat on the open terrace. Take-out is available.

L'Iguane
Carre d'Or Shopping Arcade

Quai de la République

☎ 27-88-46

Moderate

Open 9 am-11 pm; closed Sunday

During daylight hours L'Iguane is a café in the shopping arcade. Its umbrella-covered tables stand in the walkway. You can stop for croissants and café au lait, for ice cream, sandwiches and salads. When the sun goes down the chef rips open his shirt to reveal an "S"– no, not for superman, but for sushi and sashimi. Sushi platters include conch, shrimp, tuna and eel. Also delicious is the beef or tuna tataki (like carpaccio) and the vegetable rolls.

Sushi served from November through May only.

La Marine
Rue Jeanne d'Arc, La Pointe
☎ 27-70-13
Lunch and dinner; closed Sunday
Moderate

You know it's Thursday when you see scores of sailboats tied to the dock and lots of minimokes in the parking lot near La Marine. Insiders know that French shellfish arrive in St. Barts every Thursday. Oysters and mussels are the most sought after, but sardines, tuna, sole, red mullet and lobsters are also popular. Very informal.

Closed September 1-October 15.

Ines' Ghetto
Rue du Général de Gaulle
☎ 27-53-20
Inexpensive
Dinner only; closed Sunday

MC/Visa only.

Looking for a less intense and less expensive dining experience? Head to Ines' Ghetto, which is located on Gustavia's main street but is hidden from view by tropical plants. As you enter the pebbled courtyard you'll be greeted by a scene out of *Arabian Nights*. Colorful silk scarves flow from the metal roof while batiks and prints showing life in the East add counterpoint to the basic wooden tables and free-standing metal sculptures. Sink into a red pillow on a wicker chair and study the French/Creole menu, which is written on a blackboard and changes daily. A typical menu might have tartare à l'avocat (ceviche in an avocado), crab salad, seafood lasagne, BBQ ribs and chocolate mousse. The crowd is usually young and noisy, but friendly.

Eddy's Restaurant

Rue du Général de Gaulle

☎ 27 54 17

No credit cards.

Moderate

No reservations; dinner only

If Ines' is too crowded or the menu isn't appealing, head down the street to Eddy's. Eddy was the original owner of Ines', which he sold to open a similar, if slightly more upscale, eatery a few steps away. Once again, the restaurant is hidden by tropical plants in a plant-filled, tree-dotted garden topped by a thatched roof with hanging lights. Once again the menu changes to make use of the freshest ingredients.

Specialties here might include fresh conch baked in pastry, black sausage in sweet and sour sauce, and Thai shrimp or goat or chicken curry. A fun place to eat.

Saint Jean

Vincent Adam

Carenage Hill, Saint Jean Beach
☎ 27 93 22
Dinner only, 6:30 -10 pm
Expensive

Open all year.

This gourmet restaurant (often called simply "Adam") sits on a hillside overlooking the beach and town. A sign on the St. Jean-Lorient road points to the narrow dirt road that takes you to the restaurant. It isn't far and you'll spot the striped blue and green awning on a *case*. Park in the sandy lot. The restaurant retains the name and traditional French dishes of its original owner/chef, although he is no longer associated with it. The menu, which changes frequently, has many innovative dishes. Among them, a crunchy flat pancake of mashed potatoes topped with grilled salmon, pork stew with walnuts, lobster tabboule, seafood lasagne, and filet of beef with mushrooms. You can dine in the flowery garden, on the terrace that overlooks St. Jean, or inside. There is a prix-fixe menu each night.

Grande Saline

June through October hours 12-4pm only.

Grande Saline is unofficially a nudist beach.

Le Tamarin
Grande Saline
☎ 27-72-12
Lunch and dinner; closed Monday
Dinner only to 9:30
Moderate

Grande Saline is arguably the island's loveliest beach and is certainly among the least used. It has no facilities, so locals often stop for lunch at nearby Le Tamarin. It's a funky but upscale beach eatery with tables on a porch, in the garden or on the grass. Picnic-style tables on a sand patch are shaded by thatch umbrellas. You can sip a cool drink under the century-old tamarind tree that gives the restaurant its name or on a lounge chair or hammock, which are placed nearby. You can exchange quips with Cookie, the resident parrot who can hold his own in French and English.

If you are expecting hot dogs and hamburgers – fuhgedaboudit! The menu runs along the lines of carpaccios of beef and fish, chicken breast with honey and prunes, ceviche with lime and coconut or steak tartare. Apple pie and chocolate cake are good finishers. After a meal like this you have to sunbathe until you digest.

Grand Cul de Sac

Le Rivage
St. Barths Beach Hotel
Grand Cul de Sac
☎ 28-82-42
Moderate
Lunch & dinner

Le Rivage is as close to being a "comfortable neighborhood restaurant" as it gets on St. Barts. It is built on a wooden plank boardwalk which is covered by a roof and enclosed by thick, plastic, see-through curtains that are open at lunch and even at dinner when the temperature and the waves are right. The restaurant is just above the sandy beach and adjacent to the pool at the St. Barth Beach Hotel on Grand Cul de Sac Beach, one of the nicest on the island.

Non-guests eating lunch at Le Rivage can use the hotel's pool.

Not owned by the hotel, Le Rivage always has a respected local chef in its kitchen. Although nominally a French and Creole restaurant, the menu tilts south at dinner when you can start with sliced small salmon, shrimp with hot goat cheese or a tomato and mozzarella salad. Shrimp Creole, conch stew and chicken stew with curry sauce (which we ate several times) are all delicious. Lunch finds pastas, blood sausage and chunky lobster and crab salad. The staff is young and friendly. Good food and a relaxed dress code. You can smoke a cigar on the beach for dessert.

Le Colonial
Route de Saline
☎ 27-53-00
Dinner only; Amex only
Expensive

Closed Sept. 1 through Oct. 15.

One of the most attractive restaurants on St. Barts, Le Colonial is not well known because it is off the beaten track on the road from Saint Jean to Grande Saline. Set in a garden, the restaurant has a wide open feeling because it is on a covered terrace with a very high peaked roof. Its dim lighting and subdued wall hangings give it a romantic feel. The bar and cocktail areas have highly polished tables and multi-colored couches. The dining room has black lacquered tables and chairs. The decor is very dramatic.

> **◉ TIP**
>
> The chef at Le Colonial is Cambodian and the dishes are Thai, Vietnamese, Laotian and Cambodian. Look for interesting spices and lots of fish.

The Thai beef salad was enough for an entire meal, while the gingered fish rolled in a banana and seafood marmite was light and left enough room for dessert. The food is attractively served.

Marigot Bay Club

Marigot

☎ 27-75-45

Lunch and dinner; closed Monday

Moderate-Expensive

Open all year.

Marigot Bay Club is an informal restaurant just a few steps from Marigot Bay. The seafood here is as good as anywhere on the island. That's because Jean-Michel Ledee, the owner, is a working fisherman. The day's catch is the day's menu and only a few veal or chicken dishes are also available.

The lunch crowd – often wearing bathing suits with cover-ups – arrive here before or after a morning at Marigot Beach or one of the other beaches nearby. Dinner finds many diners from nearby hotels in Bermuda-style shorts or jeans. The restaurant is very informal with a long bar area and small roof-covered terrace facing the bay. Polished wood tables and director-style chairs adorn the terrace. Lobsters, grilled or baked in the shell with gruyère cheese, are most popular. Tuna and red snapper glazed with Creole sauce are flakey and delicious. Hot goat cheese on salad greens or an appetizer portion of lobster stew are great starters.

Anse Des Cayes

New Born

Closed Sundays off-season.

Anse des Cayes

☎ 27-67-07

Dinner only

Moderate

Owners Franky and David are lobster fishermen and they take great pride in the lobster dishes at their small restaurant near the Manapany Cottages Hotel. This is a terrific place to sample Creole dishes such as curried goat or shrimp and salt cod salad. A small restaurant, it has a tile floor, mauve tablecloths and wall hangings from Mexico. A large aquarium takes center stage. This informal place attracts diners from the hotel or locals.

Lunch At The Beach-St. Barts' Style

Lunch is commonly the day's main meal for European visitors and for St. Barthians. That means that a burger or hot dog, fare served on most U.S. beaches, does not cut it here. Lunch on St. Barts brings grilled meats and fish, lobster salad, pasta and good wine. To meet the demand, an unusual dining phenomenon exists on the island. Several top-notch restaurants with beachfront locations open to serve lunch and only lunch. They do not re-open for dinner, even though some are in hotels. It works something like this: The morning is spent on the beach, windsurfing or playing beach volleyball, working up an appetite and a sweat. People then head to a nearby restaurant, which has a pool adjacent to it. They take a refreshing swim, put on a t-shirt or cover-up, and sit down to a long leisurely lunch. Then they head back to the beach or home for a nap. If you want to give it a try, here are the best places to do so.

Saint Jean Beach

Filao Beach Hotel Restaurant. Lunch is served from noon until 2:30 pm. A member of the Relais & Chateaux organization, the restaurant has marble tables and a flowering cactus plant sits on each one. The lunch menu features chilled avocado soup, smoked local fish, lobster salad with asparagus, a marinated spicy chicken sandwich with beets, omelettes and salads. ☎ 27-64-84.

Le Tom Beach Hotel Restaurant-Lunch is served from noon until 2:30 pm. The menu here is similar but includes grilled meats and fish, stuffed crabs and hot as well as cold soups. ☎ 27-53-13.

Grand Cul De Sac Beach

Lafayette Club. Serves lunch from noon until 3:30 pm. This is a local institution. Business deals are clinched here and celebrity guests are entertained here. People eat here in business attire, and a chic fashion boutique is open as well. Barbecued lobster is king of the menu and, at $70, it should be. Duck, grilled fish and meats, goat cheese salad, pastas and more are menu staples. The piña coladas are legendary and potent, which you may appreciate when you see the check. Prices here are incredibly high. ☎ 27-62-51.

Le Gloriette. Serves lunch from noon until 3 pm. Not as chic as its neighbor but not nearly as pricey either, Le Gloriette serves Creole dishes such as stuffed crab, goat or chicken curry, codfish critters and lobster. No credit cards. ☎ 27-75-66.

All-Day Restaurants

As previously noted, most restaurants on St. Barts serve lunch at specific hours, then close until dinner time. What's a nosher to do? Head to one of the restaurants below. They serve from early in the morning till the wee hours – which on St. Barts is usually 11 pm.

Gustavia

Le Repaire
Rue de la République (at the port)
☎ 27-72-48
Moderate

No credit cards.

A bustling brasserie on the harbor, Le Repaire opens at 6 am when crewpersons stop by for croissants and coffee while getting their boats ready for the day. They also serve American breakfasts. By midday salads and sandwiches replace the croissants and by evening steak frites and Creole dishes take center stage. Le Repaire gets a shipment of French mussels and oysters every Thursday. They rarely make it to the weekend. An attractive stop with white-washed walls, waffle-top tables and director's chairs, it often has reggae music on tape. Pool tables and live music on weekends keep La Repaire busy till its 1 am close (the kitchen closes earlier).

La Crêperie
Rue Oscar II
Hours 7 am-11 pm; closed Sunday
Inexpensive

MC/Visa only.

With only a half-dozen tables inside and even fewer on the sidewalk, you may find yourself waiting for a table at La Crêperie. It is one of the few restaurants that serves all day from 7 am till 11 pm. At lunch you can dig into a burger or sandwich, but everyone around you will be eating a buckwheat crêpe filled with Swiss cheese, spinach and bacon or tarragon chicken, among other fillers. If you prefer to nosh or need a late afternoon pick-me-up, you can try the wheat crêpes filled with ice cream or you can have an ice cream sundae.

Saint Jean

Le Perroquet Blue

Major credit cards accepted

Neptune Shops
Hours: 9 am to 10 pm
Inexpensive

A small, clean restaurant that makes over-stuffed sandwiches with chicken, eggs, smoked fish and other items. Also crêpes and ice cream. You can eat inside or on the terrace, and take-out is available.

La Créole Restaurant and Bar

Major credit cards accepted

La Villa Créole Shopping Center
Hours: 7 am to 11 pm daily
Inexpensive

In the hub of the island's largest shopping center, this restaurant has indoor tables as well as tables on a terrace. They serve American-style food, including hot dogs, burgers, ham and cheese sandwiches, mushroom and cheese omelettes and roast chicken.

Pointe Milou (mid-island)

Le Ti St. Barth
Hours 7 am to 11 pm
Closed Monday
In Pointe Milou on the only road
Inexpensive-Moderate
A small café with a great view of this upscale residential area and the coast, Le Ti serves breakfast, lunch and dinner. House specialties are Creole dishes such as crayfish fricassee, lobster salad with Creole sauce and snail cassolette, but you'll also find hamburgers, salads and pizzas.

Picnic Fare

Want to spend the day on the beach? Pick up picnic food at the **La Rotisserie** shop nearest to your hotel. They sell roast chicken, French and local sausage, pâtés, tabbouleh, salads, sandwiches, cheeses, quiches, freshly baked bread and pastries. Pizza too. The main store is in Gustavia on Rue du Roi Oscar II (☎ 27-63-13). Branches are in Saint Jean and Point Milou. The shops in Gustavia and Saint Jean open at 7 am. The one at Point Milou opens at 5 am and serves breakfast.

Local Watering Holes

Some places take on an aura that is larger than life, especially in a place like the Caribbean where boats and yachts move from island to island. One of those places is **Le Select,** on Rue Général de Gaulle at Rue de la France, the busiest corner of Gustavia. Not much to look at, Le Select's reputation draws boat crews, young locals who drop in for a beer and dominoes after work, and just about every visitor to St. Barts, from Rockefellers to Swedish royalty.

The founder and owner Marius Stackelborough, a Swedophile, has portraits of Swedish kings on the walls along with postcards from his friends across the globe and newspaper clippings about Le Select from papers all over the world. The many languages spoken throughout the enclosed bar area make it seem like a Tower of Babel. The crowd usually spills over into the open courtyard shaded by seagrape trees. A must here is the "Cheeseburger in Paradise," named for the Jimmy Buffet song. Jimmy, who is here often, usually entertains. A must stop. Hours are Monday through Saturday, 10:30 am to 10:30 pm all year.

Diagonally across the street, the more sedate **Bar de l'Oubli** draws many of the same imbibers as Le Select. It has a much more extensive menu and its tables are covered. Better food, but not nearly as much fun. Hours are 7:30 am to 1 pm, including Sunday.

La Cave de Saint Barthelemy

French wines are considered the world's finest. **La Cave** imports wines from over 300 vintners and has 300,000 bottles in stock at all times. This warehouse (absolutely functional, not elegant) is climate-controlled to keep the wines at their optimum temperature.

Reds from Bordeaux, Burgundy and the Rhone Valley, whites, and a wide range of champagnes are sold here – by the bottle and the case. They will ship your purchase home for you (subject to duty). If you enjoy fine wines, you'll enjoy visiting the Cave. Hours: Tuesday-Friday, 9 am to noon; 3 pm to 6 pm. Saturday and Sunday, 10 am to noon. Closed Monday. ☎ 27-63-21; fax 27-87-05.

After Dark

As previously noted, St. Barts has an unusually large number of restaurants for such a small island. And they don't roll up the "rues" right after dinner the way so many Caribbean islands do. If you want to enjoy a show, dance the night away or listen to jazz at a table with a view, you can.

□ **TIP**

We'll offer some suggestions below, but to find out what's happening when you are on the island, check the daily newspaper, *Le Journal de St. Barth,* and ask your hotel concierge.

Piano Bars

Carl Gustaf (Gustavia) has great views and top-notch pianists. In season a jazz/guitar act takes over. Popular late and at sunset. ☎ 27-82-83.

L'Ananas (Gustavia) in an old restored manor house has great views and a piano man that stays till 1 am. ☎ 27-63-77.

La Mandala (Gustavia) is right next door. Tapas and drinks served from 5 pm-11 pm. Drinks and music till midnight. ☎ 27-96-96.

Guanahani (Grand Cul de Sac) has a piano in its lobby as well as a cocktail lounge. You can enjoy your drink on the nearby outer terrace as well. ☎ 27-66-60.

Manapany Cottages (Anse des Cayes) has its piano bar on the terrace adjacent to the crashing waves. ☎ 27-66-55.

Imbibing, Music, Pool, Etc.

American Bar at L'Escale Restaurant (La Pointe) stays open even after the last crust of pizza is gone. Draws a young crowd that plays backgammon and watches music videos. ☎ 27-86-07.

Jungle Café (La Pointe) is a funky spot that serves its complete menu of Thai, Chinese, Japanese and Italian dishes until it closes at midnight. Also has a popular happy hour. ☎ 27-67-29.

Le Repaire (Gustavia) stops serving at 10:30 but the bar, reggae music and billiard tables keep going till midnight. ☎ 27-72-48.

Le Select and **Bar de L'Oubli** (Rue de France, Gustavia) sit on diagonal corners and are both popular hangouts. Le Select draws the beer and burger crowd till 10:30 pm and L'Oubli draws the beer and billiard crowd till 10 pm.

Le Santa Fe (near Gouverneur Beach) has a big screen TV often tuned to U.S. sports events or international soccer matches. ☎ 27-61-04.

Topolino (Saint Jean) is an informal beachfront stop that has good jazz and reggae. Le

Pelican nearby has music till midnight. ☎ 27-70-92.

Cabaret Shows

La Banane, West Indies Café, El Sereno Hotel. ☎ 27-64-80. You can enjoy French food and stay for this loud, rowdy revue that features local singers and dancers. Or you can come for the show only.

L'Indigo, Guanahani Hotel. ☎ 27-66-60. Has a cabaret show Thursday nights and special theme dinners on several nights. There's an informal restaurant at poolside. Its barbecue and Latin nights are legendary.

Dancing (disco)

Feeling (near the Santa Fe Restaurant) is a nightclub with live music for dancing and cabaret shows at midnight. Opens at 10 pm and closes at 2 or 3 am. ☎ 27-88-67.

Le Petit Club (Gustavia) for late night dancing. It opens at 10 pm. ☎ 27-66-33.

La Licorne (Lorient) is very popular with locals. It's open only on Saturdays from 10 pm. ☎ 27-83-94.

Movie Rentals

There is no cinema theater on St. Barts, but it does have several video rental shops and they have current videos in several languages. Many hotels have TVs and VCRs as part of the furnishings. You can be a couch potato.

Tropic Video, St. Jean	☎ 27-98-85
St. Barth Video Club	☎ 27-68-39

St. Barts A To Z

Banks

Banque Française Commerciale, Rue du Général de Gaulle, Gustavia. ☎ 27-62-62. Saint Jean branch, ☎ 27-87-75. Hours: 8 am to noon and 2 pm to 3:30 pm. Closed weekends, holidays and afternoons preceding holidays.

Drinking Water

Do not drink tap water. Hotels and restaurants serve filtered water. Bottled water from Guadeloupe and France is sold here.

Electric Current

Voltage is 220 AC 60 cycles. Sockets have two round-prong outlets. U.S. appliances need converters and adapters.

French Wines

See La Cave de Saint Barthelemy, above.

Hitchhiking

Hitchhiking is very common on the island.

Hospital

Gustavia Clinic. ☎ 27-60-35.

Language

French is the official language. Some older folks speak to one another in an old Norman dialect. People working in hotels and restaurants and young people in general speak English.

Mini Markets

Closed Sundays.

Mini-Mart & Jojo in Lorient is open from 7:30 am to noon, and 2 pm to 7 pm.

Monoshop in Marigot is open from 8 am to 1 pm and again from 3 to 7 pm.

Newspaper

Daily, French and English.

NFL Withdrawal

Can't miss Monday night football or the big game on Sunday? Head to the Santa Fe restaurant at Morne Lorne (near Gouverneur Beach) for burgers, brew and football on a big screen TV.

Pharmacies

In Gustavia on Quai de la République. ☎ 27-61-82.

In Saint Jean in La Savane Commercial Centre. ☎ 27-66-61.

Physicians

There are several dentists on the island as well as a pediatrician, an opthamologist and other specialists. Your best bet is to check with the concierge. Villa renters should contact their rental agent.

Post Offices

The island's main post office is on Rue de Centenaire in Gustavia. Branches are located in

Saint Jean and Lorient. Mail from St. Barts takes two to three weeks to reach the United States.

Religious Services

In Gustavia - Roman Catholic Church on Rue du Presbitaire; Anglican Church on Rue de Centenaire.

In Lorient - Roman Catholic Church.

In Colombier - Roman Catholic Church.

Check mass times with your concierge.

Special Island Events

Contact the St. Barts Tourist Office for exact dates.

Carnival (pre-lenten celebration): Costumes, parades and the burning of the Carnival King on Ash Wednesday, usually February.

St. Barts Film Festival: Features Caribbean films in April.

The **Festival Gastronomique** lasts two weeks in April.

The **Classical & Jazz Music Festival** is held in January.

Feast Day of St. Bartholomew & Seafarers Festival takes place in August.

An **International Art Exhibit** is held in December.

Supermarket

AMC Fleurs, Gustavia Harbor. Monday, Tuesday, Thursday and Friday, 8 am to 7 pm; Wednesday 8 am to 1 pm; Saturday 8 am to 5 pm.

Take-Out Food

La Rotisseries, Gustavia. Open daily from 7 am-6:30 pm, and on Sunday, 7 am to 1 pm. In Saint Jean, hours are 7 am-7:30 pm. In Point Milou, 5 am to 10 pm (closed Monday).

Boulangeries. In Gustavia they're open Tuesday through Sunday 5 am to 11 am; In Lorient, Monday through Saturday, 8 am to noon.

Telephones

St. Barts Area Code is 590.

Calls from the U.S. are international. You must dial 011 + 590 + the number. Calling out from St. Barts to the U.S., dial 19 + 1 + area code and number.

Calls to French St. Martin are direct dial and require no area code. For calls to Dutch Sint Maarten, you must dial 3 + number.

There are public telephone booths at different points on the island. No coins are accepted. You must purchase a telecarte at the post office (Gustavia, Saint Jean, Lorient). The card can be used for local and international calls. Phone booths can be found in the shopping centers of Saint Jean, Gustavia Port, Corossol, Lorient, Colombier among others.

Time Zone

St. Barts time is one hour ahead of Eastern Standard Time. When it is 6 am in Miami, it is 7 am in St. Barts. The time is the same when the east coast is on daylight savings time. They use a 24-hour clock.

Tourist Offices

In Gustavia on Quai Général de Gaulle. ☎ 27-87-27. Hours: 8:30 am-6 pm Monday through Friday; 8:30 am to noon on Saturday.

In New York, contact the **French Tourist Board**, 444 Madison Ave., New York, NY 10022. ☎ 212/ 838-7800.

Yacht Visitors

Sailboats can anchor in Gustavia, Colombier, Public and Corossol and may pick up provisions at Loulou's Marine , ☎ 27-62-74.

Sint Maarten/ Saint Martin

*T*his is the world's smallest land mass that is home to two sovereign nations.

Peter Stuyvesant, who fought here for Holland, would be hard pressed to find much Dutch culture here today. St. Maarten, with its bustling capital Philipsburg, is a wonderful vacation destination – but it isn't a Dutch one. The southern portion of the island has the largest number of duty-free shops in the Caribbean. It has modern high-rise resort hotels, lovely beaches, a golf course, good restaurants and gambling casinos.

The French side of the island has retained more of its French culture, language and tranquility. It has grown more slowly and even its new hotels are low-rise. There are almost as many duty-free shops, but these continue to close at noon for a long leisurely lunch. And what would a slice of France be like without great food? St. Martin rivals nearby St. Barts as the gourmet capital of the Caribbean. While few Dutch people have moved here, a large number of French have emigrated in recent years. Many have opened the restaurants, cafés and bakeries that give the streets of Marigot the same aroma as that of tiny Riviera towns.

But together, the Dutch-French island offers a dynamite vacation, particularly when you add West Indian culture to the mix.

> **★ NOTE**
>
> We use "St. Martin" when referring to the island as a whole. "Sint Maarten" is used specifically for the Dutch side.

The island has 37 stunning beaches, some on the Atlantic and others on the Caribbean. The difference in the waters creates options for every type of watersport. Beach shacks stock top-rated gear for windsurfers, jet skiers and boogie boarders. They even give lessons. St. Martin's beaches retain the French tradition of topless bathing. Clothing-optional beaches exist as well. The island's central location makes it easy to take day trips to Anguilla, Saba, St. Eustatius and St. Barts. Landlubbers can play golf, tennis and sand volleyball or take a horseback ride. Hiking trails thread the island. You can pamper yourself with a seaweed massage. There are picturesque West Indian towns to explore and a lively market where you can test your bargaining skills.

After the sun sets you can enjoy a gourmet dinner or a finger lickin' one before you head to a casino or a sidewalk café to listen to calypso or reggae.

Philipsburg, the Dutch capital, and Marigot, the French one, are just 10 miles apart. The island's cultural divisions will increase your enjoyment and widen your travel horizons even as you get a great suntan.

Getting There

By Air

 International flights from the U.S. and Europe land at Princess Juliana International Airport on the island's southern coast and the Dutch side. Major U.S. carriers include American Airlines, with non-stop flights from New York (in season) and several direct flights daily through Miami and Puerto Rico. Continental Airlines and USAir also connect through Puerto Rico. Major European carriers such as AirFrance, KLM and Lufthansa land at Pointe-à-Pitre Airport in Guadeloupe.

Flights from Puerto Rico and Guadeloupe connect to commuter airlines. These include:

Air Guadeloupe	☎ 590-87-12-14
American Eagle	☎ 5995-52-040
Windward Island Airways	☎ 5995-54-230

There is a small airport, Espérance Grand Case, on the French side of Saint Martin. It can handle only commuter-size planes and inter-island flights from Guadeloupe and St. Barts.

> **◙ TIP**
>
> Make the connecting flight reservation at the same time as your long distance flight.

Entry Requirements

U.S. citizens arriving at Princess Juliana Airport or Espérance Grand Case Airport need either a valid passport, a passport with an expiration date less than five years old, an original birth certificate, or a voter registration card. The latter two also require a photo ID. A return or continuing flight ticket is also required. European Union citizens require a valid passport or a national identity card. French citizens arriving at Espérance from Guadeloupe do not need documents.

No vaccinations are required.

Money Matters

In Sint Maarten the official currency is the florin, but in reality the U.S. dollar is accepted everywhere. The same is true in Saint Martin, where the official currency is the French franc.

> ★ **DID YOU KNOW?**
>
> French francs are not accepted on the Dutch side and florins aren't accepted on the French side.

Major credit cards are accepted at hotels, restaurants and shops, as are traveler's checks. Some hotels will require a deposit by check.

Tipping

In lieu of a tip, a 10 to 15% service charge is added to your restaurant bill in both Saint Martin and Sint Maarten. It is common to leave an additional amount when the service merits it.

Getting Around

Navigating The Island

One major road (the name changes frequently) circles the island, with smaller roads leading from it to the towns and bays. Another major road cuts through the island connecting Philipsburg and Marigot. It cuts 15 minutes off the circular route's time.

Car/Jeep Rentals

 Most visitors to the island rent a car. Roads are paved and well maintained, and there is very little traffic except on the entrance roads to Philipsburg. Drive on the right side of the road as in the U.S.

Road signs are easy to read.

International car rental agencies have booths at the airport. There are many local agencies throughout the island and at major hotels.

> **⊡ TIP**
>
> You should reserve your car in advance in high season. In the off-season you might consider a local rental agency since rates will be lower and cars will be comparable. You can bargain.

Major companies include:

Avis	☎ 800-331-1084
Budget	☎ 800-472-3325
Eurocar (National)	☎ 800-328-4567
Hertz	☎ 800-654-3131

Local companies on the Dutch side include:

Adventure Car Rental	☎ 5995-43-688
Safari Rentals	☎ 5995-53-186
Sunshine Car	☎ 5995-52-684

On the French side:

Espérance Rentals, Marigot	☎ 590-87-51-09
Hibiscus Rentals, Baie Nettle	☎ 590-87-74-53
Mist Enterprises Grand Case Beach Hotel	☎ 590-85-91-32

Motorcycle & Scooter Rentals

Harley Davidson Cole Bay (Dutch)	☎ 5995-42-755
Eugene Moto Marigot (French)	☎ 590-87-13-97

Taxis

Taxis display authorization stickers. They meet flights at Princess Juliana and Espérance Airports. There are taxi stands in Philipsburg, Marigot, Grand Case and Maho. Elsewhere, taxis must be called. There is a fee schedule, but there are no meters. Fares go up 25% after 10 pm and 50% after midnight.

In Marigot	☎ 87-56-54
In Grand Case	☎ 87-75-79

In Philipsburg ☎ 22-359

┌──────────────────────────┐
│ ▣ **TIP** │
└──────────────────────────┘

Fares are not overly high but can add up, especially at night when waiting time adds to the fare.

Buses

There is no public bus system on the island but private buses run between 7 am and 7 pm. They connect towns with one another but do not go directly to beaches or bays. There are no bus stops. Just stand at the side of the road and flag it down. Very inexpensive.

Inter-Island Travel

By Plane

See Getting There *for airlines.*

Small puddle-jumpers connect Sint Maarten and St. Barts. Flights take 15 minutes and are frequent throughout the day. There are also daily flights to Saba and St. Eustatius, but these run less frequently.

Flights from Saint Martin also connect to Saint Barts and Guadeloupe. There is a $10 departure tax.

By Boat

To Anguilla: Ferries leave Marigot dock every half-hour from 8 am to 5:30 pm daily. The trip takes about 20 minutes. You need a passport or other forms of identification listed in *Entry Requirements*, above. There is a $2 departure tax.

Check on current schedules at desk.

To St. Barts: *Gustavia Express* is a ferry service that makes the crossing several times each day. It leaves from Bobby's Marina in Philipsburg on Monday, Wednesday and Friday. The trip takes one hour. It leaves from Marigot's dock on Tuesday, Thursday and Saturday. This trip takes 1½ hours. Sunday crossings only to Philipsburg. ☎ 27-77-24 to check current schedules. At this writing the adult round-trip fare from Philipsburg is $44 and $50 from Marigot. Children between the ages of two and 12 pay a third less.

Voyager I makes one crossing daily from the Marigot dock. It leaves at 8:45 am with a 5:30 pm return. Fare is $50. ☎ 87-10-68 (French side); ☎ 24-096 (Dutch side).

The Edge makes the crossing in under one hour on Tuesday, Thursday and Saturday. In season *The Edge* schedules an additional trip on Monday. Fare is $50. Leaves from Pelican Marina, Simpson Bay. ☎ 42-640, ext. 1553.

To Saba: ***The Edge*** makes this crossing in one hour on Wednesday, Friday and Sunday. Fare is $60. Leaves from Pelican Marina, Simpson Bay. ☎ 42-640, ext. 1553.

Orientation

*T*his is the smallest landmass in the world to be divided by two nations. The political division has lasted for 350 years. There is a cultural division as well. Saint Martin in the north has retained its French traditions and customs. It has the ambience of a town on the French Riviera transported to the West Indies. French is both the official language and the conversational one. It is spoken on the streets and in the hotels, restaurants and shops. It is joined in the market by the lilting English common in the Caribbean. French restaurants, cafés and bakeries are important parts of the landscape. Restaurants and shops operate on the European system, closing at midday for a leisurely lunch. Many shopkeepers and restaurateurs are recent arrivals from France.

★ DID YOU KNOW?

St. Martin is a sub-prefecture of Guadeloupe (as is St. Barts), and residents vote in both local and French national elections.

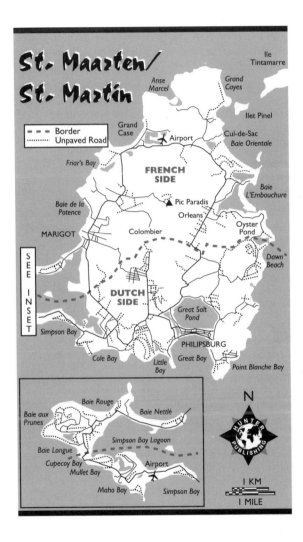

St. Maarten/
St. Martin

- - - Border
·········· Unpaved Road

Ile
Tintamarre

Anse
Marcel

Grand
Cayes

Ilet Pinel

Grand
Case

✈ Airport

Cul-de-Sac
Baie Orientale

Friar's Bay

FRENCH
SIDE

Baie
L'Embouchure

Baie de la
Potence

▲ Pic Paradis

Orleans

Oyster
Pond

MARIGOT

Colombier

Dawn
Beach

S
E
E

I
N
S
E
T

DUTCH
SIDE

Great Salt
Pond

Simpson Bay

PHILIPSBURG

Cole Bay

Little
Bay

Great Bay

Point Blanche Bay

Baie Rouge

Baie Nettlé

Baie aux
Prunes

Simpson Bay Lagoon

N

Baie Longue

Cupecoy Bay
Mullet Bay

Airport

HUNTER
PUBLISHING

Maho Bay

Simpson Bay

1 KM

1 MILE

To longtime residents, Saint Martin has become very built up, but as a visitor, you won't think so. True, there are many new hotels, but few are large. You'll appreciate the fine restaurants and shops, particularly since Marigot is a duty-free port. The beaches are largely undeveloped, with only a few offering even a water-sports center.

Sint Maarten, in the south, rushed headlong into the second half of the 20th century, becoming a tax haven, which allowed foreign investment in its tourist industry. Large resort hotels were constructed almost overnight and casinos flourished, as did duty-free shops. The southern half of the island became a major cruise ship destination.

Sint Maarten's economy boomed. It drew workers from other Caribbean islands, many of whom arrived illegally. Few people speak Dutch, although it is the official language. English is the working language and many residents speak Papiamento (idiomatic language spoken in the Dutch West Indies). Spanish is common as well. Sint Maarten might have continued to flourish but for Hurricane Luis, which hit the island in September 1995, badly damaging hotels, yachts and homes. Even the airport was closed for two months. Many hotels were closed for a year or more and even now some still remain closed. Money from Holland and other foreign sources was slower in coming here than on the French side. Perhaps it is because Sint Maarten is part of the Netherlands Antilles (with Saba, St. Eustatius, Bonaire and Curaçao) and not an integral part of Holland itself. As such, the Dutch governor is only the titular head of the government. The local legislature is the actual one.

Although a French flavor remains in the north and a Dutch one is still felt in the south, the two have blended and meshed with the West Indian culture over the past 350 years. Hence, local foods, frenetic markets and traditional festivals are celebrated with equal fervor on both sides of the imaginary border.

The political and cultural divisions will not be important to you as you explore the towns, swim at the beaches, shop in the stores or eat in the restaurants. Only casino-hoppers will have to head south.

Towns & Sites

Princess Juliana Airport

In Sint Maarten, Princess Juliana handles all international flights and the bulk of inter-island flights as well. On a south coast isthmus, it is five miles west to Marigot and six miles east to Philipsburg.

Philipsburg

The capital of Sint Maarten is built around Great Bay, a sheltered harbor that is the busiest port in the Lesser Antilles. Surprisingly small, the heart of the town is only four streets wide, restricted by the Great Salt Pond just inland. Front Street edges the coast and is the busiest street in town. It is lined with duty-free shops, restaurants of all types, small inns and two casinos. Back Street, the second block, is a less crowded version of Front Street. The streets are connected by narrow alleys called "steegjes," which have shops and nite clubs as well. Philipsburg is bustling during the day and night.

Front Street is "Vorstraat" in Dutch. And Back Street is "Achterstraat."

Simpson Bay Lagoon

This large lagoon is rimmed by narrow isthmuses. Part of it is Dutch and it is the busiest watersports center for the south side of the island. The French side, called Baie Nettle, has a series of moderately priced hotels. Simpson Bay Lagoon's eastern tip forms the Port La Royale Marina in Marigot.

Maho Bay

Adjacent to the airport, the village at Maho Bay is the heart of Sint Maarten. It has several resort complexes, good restaurants, two shopping malls and two casinos. Surrounded by vacation villas, Maho is the local hangout for Americans. It has a beach strip.

Mullet Bay

The pride of Sint Maarten, Mullet Bay was dominated by an upscale villa resort built around the island's only golf course. Badly damaged, the resort stood mute until mid-1997 when renovations began. Only the golf course was in operation as we went to print. The town centered around the golf facility and looked like a ghost town with hardly any shops open. Check on progress. Maho Bay, Mullet Bay and Cupecoy Bay, adjacent to one another, have beach strips.

Just west of Maho.

Marigot

The capital of French Saint Martin is a delightful town with two hubs. The Port La Royal Marina is enclosed on three sides by upscale shops, gourmet restaurants and charming cafés. Lots of small sailboats and motorboats anchor here. This is the "French" hub in town. Two blocks away, the Place du Marché on Marigot Bay is the site of the West Indian flea market, the tourist office, a few upscale French restaurants and a far larger number of moderately priced West Indian eateries where local

La Royal Marina is on the lagoon.

bands play each night. Ferries leave from the dock for Anguilla and St. Barts. This is the "West Indian" hub in town. Rue Charles de Gaulle and Rue de la République are the two most important shopping streets in Marigot.

Grand Case

This is a picturesque village with many traditional-style homes and restored Creole mansions that house fine restaurants. Boulevard Grand Case is often called the Caribbean's Restaurant Row. Good hotels and a wide crescent-shaped beach are here as well.

Orient Bay

The beach at Orient Bay is the longest on the island. Hurricane Luis made it wider – a giant plus since this clothing-optional beach is crowded with beachfront restaurants, watersport centers, and even a nudist camp. Topless bathing is the norm on the island but many people do go nude here. The hillsides around the bay house hotels and villa communities. The action starts early and ends late.

Terres Basses

A lowland area that joins Cupecoy Bay (Dutch) and the beautiful Baie Longue, Baie aux

Prunes and Baie Rouge on the French side of the border monument. Many upscale residential communities are here, as is La Samanna, the island's finest resort.

Western Border.

Oyster Pond Bay

A stunning bay that is split by that imaginary border. It has fine resorts on both sides as well as an active marina. The bay is encircled by hills and has only a narrow outlet to the Atlantic. The waters are so calm that it looks like a pond.

Eastern Border.

A Brief History

The island now known as Saint Martin/Sint Maarten was spotted by Columbus during his second voyage in 1493. The date, November 11, was the Feast Day of St. Martin of Tours, after which the island was named. But Columbus made no attempt to colonize the island. The early inhabitants of the small islands in the Lesser Antilles were peaceful Arawak Indians. They were followed by the fierce Caribs, another South American tribe that took no prisoners – European or Indian. The Caribs referred to the land mass as "Sualougia," a place to get salt, a resource that proved to be key to its later colonization.

By the 1600s, Spanish, French and Dutch pirates and navies roamed through these waters looting at will. The Dutch took note of the vast salt ponds on the southern shore. They needed salt to preserve the herrings they brought back to Holland and so they claimed the island in 1631. They built a fort on the western tip of Great Bay. Nonetheless, the Spanish overran the fort and staked their claim to the island by building a fort on Pointe Blanche, the eastern tip of the bay. During this time, the French staked their claim to the northern part of the island.

In an effort to regain the island, the Dutch attacked from Curaçao (led by Peter Stuyvesant, then governor of the Dutch possessions). Stuyvesant fought valiantly, but he was unsuccessful. This was just a tiny battle, but it was part of the 80 Years War between Spain and Holland.

★ DID YOU KNOW?

Stuyvesant lost a leg during this battle, which earned him the nickname Pegleg, a name that followed him when he became governor of New Amsterdam, now New York.

Although victorious, the Spanish decided to abandon the island and released the Dutch and

French prisoners they held. The prisoners determined to stay on the island and encouraged colonization by their countrymen. Over the years, neither side could gain the upperhand and finally they decided to share the island.

Island Legend

An island legend says that the French/Dutch border was set in a walking race. A Dutchman and a Frenchman stood back to back and set off in opposite directions to walk around the island till they met. The Dutchman was slower because he was fat or he stopped often to drink gin (take your pick). No matter, the island was divided with the French retaining 21 square miles in the north and the Dutch with 16 square miles in the south.

Although the above legend makes for interesting reading, it's more likely that the majority of land was given to the French due to the larger French naval presence in the area. The border has remained firm for 350 years, although claims were made until 1816. The formal border remained unmarked until a commemorative stone was placed there in 1948.

Sugar cane plantations were established on the island in the late 1700s and slaves were brought in to work in the fields and in the houses. Sugar was the sole economic factor on the island, and when slavery was abolished (French side 1848, Dutch side 1863), the economy collapsed. The former slaves remained on the island and intermarriages created the predominant Creole culture.

In the 1940s Princess Juliana Airport was built as the Dutch side became a tax haven and duty-free port. Foreign investments in the tourist industry created resort hotels, casinos, and shops almost overnight. Great Bay became the largest port in the Lesser Antilles and the booming economy lured immigrants from nearby islands looking for work. Hurricane Luis in September 1995 put a major crimp in the economy with many people unemployed for long periods of time. St. Maarten is now part of the Netherlands Antilles, along with Curaçao, Bonaire, Saba and St. Eustatius.

The French side, also a duty-free port, did not encourage foreign investment and thus developed more slowly. The difference in pace remains till this day. St. Martin is part of the French Overseas Department governed through Guadeloupe. Citizens here vote in French national elections as well as local ones.

Sunup To Sundown

When you imagine what your days on St. Martin will be like, think water. The island offers the turquoise waters of the Caribbean, the rolling waves of the Atlantic and a tranquil lagoon as well. Each is a water playground and the wilder the watersport, the better. Snorkeling, windsurfing, waterskiing, sailing, jet skiing, wave running, sports fishing and parasailing are all readily accessible. There are a score of exciting dive spots nearby and well-organized trips to each. You can take a day sail to an uninhabited cay nearby for a picnic and snorkeling over a pristine coral reef, or you can spend a day swimming in the waters of nearby Anguilla or St. Barts.

Then think sand. There are more than 30 beaches on the coves and bays that mark the island's coastline. If the sand were laid end to end it would reach over 10 miles. And, the beaches offer options. Some are short patches wedged between rocky cliffs and others appear endless – velvety white sand dotted with sea-grape and palm trees. While the beach at Orient Bay is a blur of activity, the strip at Baie Lounge is tranquil with only a local entrepreneur to sell soft drinks and rent lounge chairs.

Topless bathing is the norm on the French side of the island and Orient Beach is officially clothing-optional. Other beaches are clothing-optional, but not officially. Swimmers on the Dutch side tend to keep their bikinis on.

Landlubbers might enjoy the 18-hole golf course oceanside at Mullet Bay.

In recent years St. Martin has taken steps to preserve its environment. Trails that were used by farmers during the Colonial era have been reclaimed and new trails allowing access to the very top of the island have been added. There are organized hikes. A marine and coastal reserve has been created to protect part of the island's coral reef. A private organization has carved out a seven-acre park that has hiking trails and all kinds of tropical vegetation.

Bridge Alert!

There is one main road that circles the island. At two points there are bridges that are raised for marine traffic. At Simpson Bay, the bridge is raised at 11 am and at 6 pm to allow access between Simpson Lagoon and the Caribbean Sea. On Sandy Ground Road, the bridge is raised at 7:30 am and at 5:30 pm for access between the lagoon and the Atlantic Ocean near Marigot. Auto traffic stops for 10 minutes each time.

There are two exciting capitals to explore – one bustling and the other laid back. And there are picturesque villages with traditional Creole buildings and gourmet restaurants to visit. There are even museums.

The shopping here is exceptional and duty-free in both capitals. Jewelry, china, imported resort wear, leathers and cameras are all good buys.

You'll be so active that you'll hardly have time to finish the latest thriller.

French-Side Beaches

Since there are beaches on every part of the island, en route to them you'll also be exploring tiny West Indian hamlets with names like Cripple Gate, Pigeon Tree Hill and Colombier.

All beaches on the island are open to the public, even those that house deluxe resorts. There is normally a path to the beach that bypasses the hotel. Some hotels charge a nominal fee for the use of changing facilities and higher fees for lounge chairs and watersports gear. Some hotels do not permit non-guests to use hotel facilities, even for a fee. Undeveloped beaches frequently have locals that rent lounge chairs and umbrellas, and sell cold drinks. Some have "lolos," or beach shacks that sell barbecued chicken, ribs and lobster.

⚠ WARNING

Keep in mind that topless bathing is the norm at pools and beaches on the French side and several beaches are clothing-optional. If you are traveling

with children you might like to
explain this cultural difference
or you might prefer to avoid it.

Generally, the beaches on the French side are
cleaner and less developed since many coves
and bays do not have hotels on them. Virtually
every beach on the Dutch side has a high-rise
hotel or villa development on it.

Orient Bay Beach

On the island's northeast coast, Orient Beach
disproves the generalization. It is a whirlwind
of activity both in the water and on the sand. It
is crowded and noisy and it is "the place" on the
island where the well-tanned and well-toned go
to be seen. And seen they are, since this is a
clothing-optional beach and many people take
the option, particularly at the southern end
which fronts the naturalist camp (see
Accommodations).

While Hurricane Luis washed sand off many
island beaches, it actually widened Orient
Beach. Crescent-shaped and over 1½ miles
long, the beach has been divided into sections
by beachfront restaurants and watersports
rental kiosks. These restaurants are popular
day and night, and have indoor and outdoor
tables. Among them are Bikini Beach (Spanish
food), Kakao (pizza), Kon Tiki (French), Coco
Beach (international), and Waikiki (French).

Each has a parking lot. Beach volleyball and paddleball games are hard fought, and the turquoise water is dotted with windsurfers and sunfloats. You can rent a lounge chair but will feel comfortable with your own blanket to sit on and picnic lunch as well. Several hotels and villa resorts are near Orient Bay (see *Accommodations*).

Baie Longue, Baie Des Prunes & Baie Rouge

A trio of stunning beaches edge the sea on Terres Basses, the lowland area near the French-Dutch border.

Baie Longue (Long Bay), the most westerly of the three, is the longest and arguably the most beautiful beach on the island. The deluxe La Samanna resort is built on the hillside above this beach. The area that fronts the resort has been landscaped but the rest of the beach has only seagrape trees and tropical plants growing untamed. It's a terrific beach for swimming and snorkeling. No food or gear rentals. There is a path from the parking lot.

Look for the road sign to La Samanna.

You can hike from the northern end of Long Bay to Baie Aux Prunes (Plum Beach) by walking around Pointe du Canonner, which juts out into the bay and is the most westerly point on the island. Plum Bay is totally undeveloped, although there are residential communities on

The main road sign, "Baie Aux Prunes," is quite faded.

the hills surrounding it. This bay gets rolling waves, and young surfers congregate to test their skills at the northern end near Bird's Cliffs. It is so secluded that nude bathing is common as well. No food or rentals. There's an access trail from the parking lot. Look for the fence.

Driving east for one mile you'll see the Baie Rouge (Red Beach) turnoff and a sandy parking lot often filled with mini-vans just beyond it. This is the most popular beach for local tour operators. "David's Hole," at the northern end, is a popular snorkeling spot and it has an interesting coral reef. There are food and lounge chair rental kiosks, but picnic food would probably be your best bet.

Cul De Sac, The Cays & Off-Shore Islands

Cul de Sac is not the most beautiful beach on the island but it is at the heart of the marine reserve and serves as the kick-off point for boat rides to offshore islands and secluded surfing beaches reached by a coastal trail. Cul de Sac's turquoise waters often have fishing boats bobbing in them. The catch of the day comes in very early. Nearby, you'll see kite and model plane flyers gather on the dark sand beach waiting for one of the wooden boats that make the run to Ilet Pinel in five minutes. Uninhabited, it has a pristine coral reef. Bring your own snorkel gear, food and water. Bigger boats make the run to Tintamarre Island, which has excellent snorkeling and scuba diving. A deserted airstrip is right off the beach and you'll see goats and turtles. Organized scuba trips come to Tintamarre.

Grand Case Beach

If taking a leisurely swim or a jog along the beach works up your appetite then head to Grand Case Beach. Not only are there a dozen gourmet eateries overlooking the shore, but directly on the sand are the best "lolos" on the island. These beach shacks (now much sturdier) serve the best barbecued ribs, chicken and lobster you've ever eaten. Inexpensive too.

Many "lolos" were destroyed by Hurricane Luis and not rebuilt.

Baie De L'Embouchure & Plage Du Galion

These secluded beaches share a cove within the marine reserve. The government has established mooring sites here to avoid damage to the cove's pristine coral reef. The tree-lined arc at L'Embouchure (Coconut Grove), preferred by surfers and snorkelers, has food and watersports rental shacks. At the northern end of the cove, Galion Beach is hardly developed. Its waters are protected by the offshore reef, mak-

The road to this cove is unpaved but easy to navigate.

ing the waters calm enough for young children. No food or rentals at this writing.

Other French-Side Beaches

Friar's Beach sits between Marigot and Grand Case. Good snorkeling beach with "lolos." Look for "La Savanne" turnoff.

Anse Marcel: Calm waters that front Le Meridien Hotel and Marina. Hotel permits rentals of lounge chairs and gear. Restaurant at the beach.

Baie Nettle: This ocean-side beach is on the isthmus connecting Marigot and Terres Basses. Lots of moderately priced hotels here.

Dutch-Side Beaches

Dawn Beach-Oyster Pond

The paved road to Dawn Beach and Oyster Pond resembles a roller coaster and the beaches are worth every pothole. Dawn Beach is stunning, surrounded by mountains, and many consider it the best snorkeling beach on the island. Refreshments and rentals. Oyster Pond has only a small beach that lures surfers. It also has a marina.

Hermit crab races held here.

Cupecoy Beach

Cupecoy looks like the beach on picture post-cards. Lined with sandstone cliffs, it doesn't have one long strip but several small coves. Follow the footpaths that connect the coves. Some are very secluded and many are clothing-optional. Many gay locals and visitors head here as well. Good snorkeling and surfing when the wind is up. Refreshments and rentals.

Maho & Mullet Bays

Maho Beach is long and has deep white sand. It can get crowded because Maho Beach Hotel has 600 rooms. The roar in your ears is not the water but the airplanes landing at Princess Juliana Airport adjacent to the beach. You can easily walk to Mullet Bay. This is a palm tree-lined strip that fronts the golf course and villas that are being reconstructed. Lots of surfers.

Simpson Bay & Lagoon

Simpson Bay is home to a small group of fisher-men that live in traditional Creole *cases* (houses). There are also several resort hotels. The lagoon is the busiest watersports center on the Dutch side of the island. Waterskiing, wind-surfing, jet skiing and sailing are only a few of the options. Lots of watersports rentals and food.

Other Dutch-Side Beaches

Great Bay: On the western edge of Philipsburg, Great Bay beach has calm waters and watersports rentals. Windsurfing is very popular.

Near Fort Amsterdam

Little Bay: At the tip of the western peninsula and fronting the Divi Little Bay Resort, this is a narrow strip but good for swimming.

Sights

Philipsburg

This early settlement on Sint Maarten's southern coast became the capital of the Dutch colony in 1733. Led by Scotsman John Philips, the settlement was perfectly located between a large protected harbor (Great Bay) and a vast saltern (Great Salt Pond). It was the saltern that provided the impetus for the settlement (the Dutch needed salt to preserve the fish they carried back to Holland). The town was built on a sandy strip parallel to the bay.

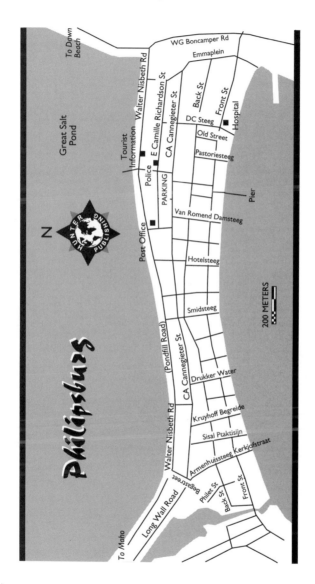

The Saltern, in use till 1949, is home to herons and migrating birds and partly filled in by landfill. Its location has restricted the growth of Philipsburg so that the heart of the city is less than a half-dozen streets wide. Two of those streets, **Front Street** (Vorstraat) and **Back Street** (Achterstraat), parallel to the bay and the small alleys that connect them (steegjes) are commercial centers with fine boutiques offering goods at duty-free prices.

Philipsburg, although damaged by hurricanes, has managed to retain its Colonial Dutch and West Indian architecture. Many of the shops are located in renovated Colonial buildings painted in typical pastels and with gingerbread (fretwork) designs on the wooden eaves, porches and rooftops. One of the best examples of Colonial architecture is the **Pasasgrahan Inn**, on the east end of Front Street. The oldest inn on the island, it was once a royal guest house that hosted Queen Wilhelmina when she visited the island. The most famous building in town is **The Courthouse** on Front Street at Wathey Square, where the dinghies from cruise ships in the harbor drop and pick-up passengers. Not in Colonial style, the white and green building dates to 1793. Renovated several times, most recently in 1994, the building has served as the local council hall, a weigh station, post office, jail and fire station. Today it functions as the court.

Another interesting stop, the **SIMARTIN Museum**, opened in 1989. It provides a historical and geological record of the island and its people. The small museum has a permanent collection, changing exhibits and beautiful antique maps. #7 Spectgjens Arcade. ☎ 24917. Small entrance fee. Hours: Monday through Saturday, 10 am to 4 pm.

Even if you aren't a shopper, you should walk along **Old Street**, a gated street filled with shops that connects Front and Back Streets.

Two forts built in the Colonial period are on the peninsulas guarding Great Bay. On the west, **Fort Amsterdam**, built in 1631, is the oldest Dutch fort in the Caribbean. In spite of its strategic position, commanding the harbor, the fort was captured by the Spanish two years later. The Dutch, led by Peter Stuyvesant, tried unsuccesfully to recapture it. It was here that Stuyvesant lost a leg before he went on to became governor of New Amsterdam (now New York). Fort Amsterdam stands on Little Bay Peninsula, a 20-minute walk from Front Street. Ruins of the **Spanish-built fort** are visible on Pointe Blanche on the eastern shore of the bay.

The fort is near the tennis courts at the Divi Resort.

Marigot

Philipsburg is a typical West Indian town much like Charlotte Amalie in St. Thomas. Marigot, on the other hand, is more like a town on the French Riviera transplanted to the Caribbean. It was not so long ago that Marigot was a sleepy fishing village, but it has renovated its lovely

"Marigot" is a French West Indian word.

old houses and put chic duty-free shops in some of them. Its marina, **Port La Royale**, is a handsome complex that comes alive each morning with schooners unloading produce for the market and visitors boarding sailboats for a day of diving. The streets are filled with sidewalk cafés and the aroma of baking baguettes, warm croissants and café au lait. As many people speak French as lilting Caribbean English.

Located on the island's western shore, the French selected the townsite because of the large bay encircled by hills that offer protection from the winds. But what is now Marigot Bay looked more like a swamp then, hence the name "Marigot," which means "spot from which rain water does not drain off and forms marshy pools." Almost immediately the colony was under attack by the English from nearby Anguilla. The French decided to build a fort, **St. Louis,** on a hill commanding the harbor. Although the British did manage to overrun the fort and settlement, gradually the attacks stopped. The fort was abandoned but has recently been restored and is an interesting spot to visit if only for the fantastic views. It's a 10-minute hike from the dock. The views are great. (You can also drive to Fort St. Louis.)

Marigot has expanded rapidly and, much to the regret of old-timers, the area near Fort St. Louis and north of the dock has several new residential communities and even a U.S.-style shopping center. But these areas are of little interest to visitors.

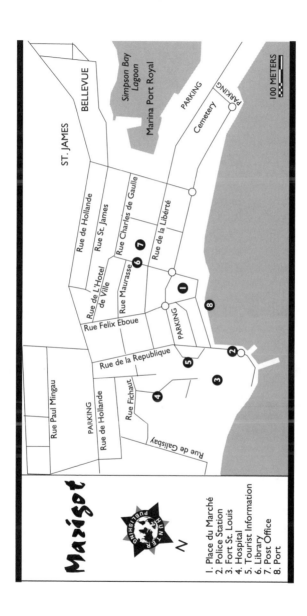

Marigot

N

NUTMEG PUBLISHING

1. Place du Marché
2. Police Station
3. Fort St. Louis
4. Hospital
5. Tourist Information
6. Library
7. Post Office
8. Port

100 METERS

BELLEVUE

ST. JAMES

Simpson Bay Lagoon

Marina Port Royal

PARKING

Cemetery

PARKING

Rue de Hollande

Rue St. James

Rue Charles de Gaulle

Rue de la Libérté

Rue de L'Hotel de Ville

Rue Maurasse

Rue Felix Eboue

PARKING

Rue de la Republique

Rue Paul Mingau

PARKING

Rue de Hollande

Rue Fichaut

Rue de Gallisbay

It's the downtown area that has all the energy, bordered by Port La Royale Marina (south) to Rue de la République (north) and the harbor walk of Rue de la Liberté, the dock and market square (west) and Rue de Hollande (east) that is the main road to Grand Case. Bursting at the seams with places to eat and party, scores of shops that sell designer duds, jewelry, perfumes and wines, Marigot's small streets are its lure. Don't miss the **market,** in operation on Wednesdays, Fridays and Saturdays. At the dock, its kiosks are filled with fruits and vegetables, fish, clothing and handicrafts. It's a slice of life on Saint Martin and it isn't strictly for tourists.

History buffs will enjoy the **Musée de Saint Martin**, often called "On the Trail of the Arawaks." Set in a two-story building, it details the island's history from pre-Columbian times to the present. It has pottery, old maps and photos, descriptions of burial sites and practices, and other interesting exhibits. Everything is described in both English and French. The second floor is an art gallery with works by local artists and monthly exhibits. The museum works with the Hope Estate, a dig that seeks to discover early artifacts. Entrance fee. Hours: 9 am to 1 pm and 3 pm to 7 pm. Closed Sundays. ☎ 29-22-84. Near the marina on Sandy Ground Road.

Grand Case

French Saint Martin and Saint Barts vie for "the best dining in the Caribbean" title. Inexplicably, it is this tiny fishing village on the island's northwestern shore that has the "hottest" restaurants on this island. Its main street runs for one mile and on virtually every inch of that mile stands a top-notch restaurant. With European-trained chefs in their kitchens, they serve French, Creole, Italian, Vietnamese and Indonesian dishes in elegant surroundings. Many are housed in restored Creole houses, which give the town a quaint, picturesque appeal. The gourmet restaurants are joined by the famed "lolos," beach shacks, where local cooks serve fabulous barbecued chicken, ribs and lobster, and such Caribbean specialties as plantains, rice and peas, and johnnycakes. On alternating Saturdays year-round you can stand on Grand Case Beach and watch sailing races between local fishermen in old fishing boats and their friendly Antillean rivals. Anguilla is visible on the horizon. Espérance Airport, which has inter-island flights, is near town as well.

Colombier & Orleans

For a peek at what St. Martin looked like 50 years ago, head to Colombier, a tiny hamlet between Marigot and Grand Case and Orleans, farther to the north. Colombier is pastoral, with goats and cows grazing behind old stone walls. Its one street is lined with typical Creole houses, surrounded by flowering gardens and painted in a variety of pastel shades. You can pick up the Sentier des Crêtes hiking trail to Paradise Peak from here as well as from Orléans, another traditional hamlet that was the site of the first French settlement on the island.

Paradise Peak (Pic Paradis)

Standing just under 1,500 feet high, this is the island's highest and greenest point. Moisture-laden clouds must drop their rain here to cross this range, so the area is enveloped in tropical growth. Views are stunning and include both Marigot and Philipsburg and the nearby islands of St. Barts, Anguilla, Saba and St. Eustatius. The hiking trail to the peak heads north from Colombier or south from Orleans. You can also drive most of the way up. Look for the turnoff between Marigot and Grand Case. Contact Action Nature for trail maps, ☎ 590-87-97-87.

Butterfly Farm

Kids will love this landscaped garden, covered with netting, that is home to over 600 butterfly species. You can visit between 9 am and 5 pm daily. The farm is on Galion Beach Road. Don't forget your camera. There are fish ponds, turtles, iguanas and birds as well. ☎ 590-87-31-21.

Sint Maarten Zoo

North of the Great Salt Pond, this modern three-acre zoo houses over 35 species of rare and endangered animals and birds native to the Caribbean and South America. The reptile collection and walk-through aviaries are highlights. On Arch Road, Madame Estate. Hours: Monday through Friday, 9 am to 5 pm; weekends 10 am to 6 pm. Madame Estate is a growing residential area near Philipsburg and offers another slice of Sint Maarten life.

Water-Based Sports Action

Day sails and snorkeling at nearby islands, scuba dives for beginners and experts, deep-sea fishing and windsurfing – all are well organized here. Check your hotel watersports center and the highly regarded operators below.

Scuba Diving

There are over 30 dive sites near St. Martin in both the Atlantic and the Caribbean. The water averages 70°F year-round and the visibility is excellent. There are not many deep drop-offs, but there are several wrecks and pristine coral reefs with marine life to explore. There are no organized beach dives. Night dives and expert instruction is available if you're looking for certification.

The wreck of the 133-foot British frigate ***Proselyte*** is the most popular dive here. Near Fort Amsterdam, it sank in 1801. Visible from the surface, snorkelers can enjoy it too. **Hens and Rocks**, off Pointe Blanche, with one large rock and two small ones, is also popular. It has a 70-foot drop-off. **Tintamarre Island**, off the coast near French Cul-de-Sac, has diving in its sheltered coves.

Scuba Shop ☎ 590-87-48-01
Capt Oliver's, Oyster Pond (French)

Red Coral Divers ☎ 590-87-74-38
Grand Case (French)

Blue Ocean Divers ☎ 590-87-89-73
Nettle Bay (French)

Leeward Island Divers ☎ 599-5-43-320
Simpson Bay (Dutch)

Ocean Explorers ☎ 599-5-42-557
Simpson Bay (Dutch)

Trade Winds Dive Center ☎ 559-5-75-176
Great Bay Marina (Dutch)

Watersports Rentals

Chances are that your hotel's waterfront rental center will have the equipment you want, but there are some centers that are outstanding and they are on the beaches where the equipment can be put to maximum use. Rental gear includes jet skis, wave runners, waterskis, skurf kneeboards, Big Bananas, canoes, kayaks, pedalboats, paddleboats, boogie boards, surfboards and fun boards.

On the French side, contact:

Orient Watersports Orient Bay	☎ 590-27-48-42
Meridian Watersports Anse Marcel	☎ 590-87-67-90
Pro Aquatique Raiders Cul de Sac	☎ 590-87-44-99
Tropical Wave Galion Beach	☎ 590-87-37-21
Nico Watersports Nettle Bay	☎ 590-87-20-59

On the Dutch side of the island, try:

Pelican Watersports Simpson Bay	☎ 599-5-42-640
Westport Watersports Simpson Bay	☎ 599-5-42-557

Windsurfing

Extremely popular on the island. **Nathalie Simon Windsurfing Club** on Orient Bay gives lessons. ☎ 590-87-48-16. Also try:

Blue Ocean, Nettle Bay	☎ 590-87-89-73
Windy Reef, Galion Beach	☎ 590-87-08-37

Snorkeling & Day Sails

If you have your own snorkel gear you can head to island beaches with near-shore reefs to enjoy the coral and marine life. Snorkel gear is easy to rent. Beaches with good snorkeling include Dawn Beach, Mullet Bay Beach, Plum Beach, Simpson Bay, Orient Beach and Pinel Island near Grand Cul de Sac.

Snorkeling is often combined with a relaxing day sail to an uninhabited cay nearby (half-day) or to St. Barts and Anguilla (full day).

White Octopus (to St. Barts) Bobby's Marina	☎ 599-5-24-096
Santino (to Anguilla) Pelican Watersports	☎ 599-5-42-640
Blue Ocean, Nettle Bay	☎ 590-87-89-73
Golden Eagle Great Bay Marina	☎ 599-5-30-068
Ocean Explorers Simpson Bay	☎ 599-5-44-357
Inspiration, Bobby's Marina	☎ 599-5-71-472

Octoplus, Grand Case   ☎ 590-87-20-62

Meridien Watersport   ☎ 590-87-67-90
Anse Marcel

Yacht Charters

The Moorings   ☎ 800-521-1126
Captain Oliver's, Oyster Pond

Tradewind Yachts   ☎ 599-5-42511
Simpson Bay Yacht Club

Sunsail, Oyster Pond   ☎ 800-327-2276

Nicholson Yacht Charters   ☎ 800-662-6066

*Make arrange-
ments long before
your arrival.*

Deep-Sea Fishing

Captained charters go out for half a day, a full day or longer. Dolphin, kingfish, sailfish, blue marlin, tuna and wahoo are the catches. Contact:

Captain Oliver's, Oyster Pond   ☎ 5995-70031

Get Hooked   ☎ 590-87-46-89

Soleil de Minuit, Oyster Pond ☎ 590-87-34-66

Leeward Island Divers   ☎ 599-54-3320
Simpson Bay

Jet Skiing/Parasailing/Sailing

Kon Tiki Watersports Orient Beach	☎ 590-87-46-89
Bikini Watersports Orient Beach	☎ 590-87-43-19
Jet Caraibes Explorer Nettle Bay	☎ 590-87-18-83
Pelican Watersports Simpson Bay	☎ 599-5-42640

Seaworld Explorer

If you don't scuba dive, you can still explore the stunning coral reefs and unusual marine life in the waters near St. Martin. The *SeaWorld Explorer* is an advanced glass-bottomed boat. The lower level is submerged and you can see the underwater world through the large glass windows. It's fun for children since staff members dive nearby and feed the fish and eels to draw them toward the *Explorer*. It is air-conditioned and the talks are in English. Leaves daily from Grand Case Pier. Fee: $30 adults, $20 children ages 2-12. ☎ 599-5-24078.

Land-Based Sports Action

Golf

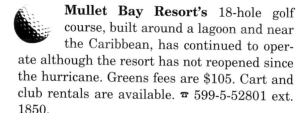

Mullet Bay Resort's 18-hole golf course, built around a lagoon and near the Caribbean, has continued to operate although the resort has not reopened since the hurricane. Greens fees are $105. Cart and club rentals are available. ☎ 599-5-52801 ext. 1850.

Trees and greens damaged by salt are just coming back to bloom.

Horseback Riding

The island offers trail rides for beginners to experienced riders along beaches and off the beaten track. Lessons given. Champagne rides for two and full moon beach rides too.

Caid & Isa, Anse Marcel	☎ 590-87-45-70
OK Corral, Oyster Pond	☎ 590-87-40-72
Bayside Riding Club (between Orient Bay & Galion Beach	☎ 590-87-36-64
Lucky Stables, Cole Bay	☎ 599-5-45255
Horsen' Around, Almond Grove	☎ 599-5-48728

Mountain Biking

Popular for pleasure and for competition. Mountain biking clubs exist and they organize group rides. Near Marigot, the Pass Partout Club and, near Princess Juliana Airport, the Friendly Mountain Biking Association organize races and rides. Contact for clubs and rentals:

Frog Legs Cyclery ☎ 590-87-05-11

Tri-Sport ☎ 599-5-54384

Fitness & Spa Services

Many of the larger hotels have fitness centers with treadmills, life cycles and Nautilus machines. If yours does not, head to:

Le Privilège Spa, Anse Marcel, ☎ 590-87-38-38, which has a well-equipped gym with instructors and a spa facility that includes several types of massage, whirlpool baths and a beauty salon.

Peter's Health Spa, Maho Beach Hotel, ☎ 599-5-52115, ext. 4951, offers exercise classes, cardiovascular and weight equipment, massages, body wraps and beauty treatments.

Tennis, Racquetball & Squash

There are tennis courts at many hotels, but squash and racquetball courts are found only at two neighboring hotels in Anse Marcel. **Le Panoramic Privilège Hotel and Spa** welcomes non-guests (☎ 590-87-38-38), as does **Le Meridien Hotel** (☎ 590-87-33-33). Fees vary and are usually charged by the hour. Other choices for tennis:

Guests have priority.

Hotel Mont Vernon	☎ 590-87-62-00
Hotel Laguna Beach	☎ 590-87-91-75
Hotel Simpson Beach	☎ 590-87-54-54
Nettle Bay Beach Club	☎ 590-87-68-68

French.

Great Bay Beach Hotel	☎ 599-5-22446
Little Bay Beach Resort	☎ 599-5-22333
Maho Beach Hotel	☎ 599-5-52115
Oyster Bay Beach Club	☎ 599-5-22206
Pelican Resort & Casino	☎ 599-5-42503

Dutch.

Hiking

Abandoned to goats and sheep for many years, more than 25 miles of hiking trails cross the island from side to side, leading to stunning viewpoints that offer an upclose look at mango trees, corossol trees, ancient plantation ruins and tiny hummingbirds. All the trails, which have been redefined or newly created, are marked. You can hike to Paradise Peak, the highest point on the island.

📺 TIP

You'll need sturdy shoes, a hat and lots of water.

For hiking trail maps, contact:

Action Nature	☎ 590-87-97-87
AGRP (Assc. of Guides Pedestre)	☎ 590-29-20-20

For group hikes:

Fun Raid Tour	☎ 590-87-59-24
Heritage Foundation	☎ 599-5-23379
Rising Sun Tours	☎ 590-87-14-22

Eden Park

This private nature park covers eight acres near Friar's Beach with walking paths and local flora and fauna. The park in Morne Emile, in the hills near La Savane, was opened in 1997. ☎ 590-29-28-32 for hours and driving directions.

Beach Volleyball

You think Karch Karai takes this game seriously. Wait till you see the game here! Big time games on Friar's Beach, Orient Beach, Galion Beach, Great Bay Beach and Mullet Bay Beach.

St. Martin Beach Volleyball ☎ 590-87-79-73

Shop Till You Drop

Island t-shirts hit the shopping nail right on the head. One says, "Not all treasure on St. Martin is buried" and another, "My daughter went to St. Martin and all I got was a 14k gold ring with an oval sapphire surrounded by diamonds." Need we say more?

For many visitors to the island, shopping is as big a lure as the sun and sand. If you are one such person, you won't be disappointed. Front Street in Philipsburg has more shops than Charlotte Amalie in St. Thomas and there are also fine shops in Marigot and in Maho Bay Village. Over 500 shops, along with flea markets and art galleries, are scattered throughout the island. You'll find all of the usual outlets familiar to Caribbean shoppers – Little Switzerland, Colombian Emeralds, Boolchands and Sparkys – but the political division has made for unique specialties. Dutch-side shops feature blue and white Delftware, Edam and Gouda cheeses and sausages, pea soup and Dutch beer. Those on the French side counter with French porcelains, Brie and Camembert cheeses and French wines and perfumes. You'll find many of the same shops in all three locations. Generally, Marigot's shops feature more designer fashions and resortwear and those in Philipsburg have more cameras and electronics.

Best buys include jewelry, watches, crystal, cameras, cigars, flatware, linens, leathers and fine fashions.

> **◻ TIP**
>
> If you are planning to buy cameras, watches or electronic equipment, check prices before leaving home. Some camera/electronic shops give "discounts" if you pay cash.

Since all the shops in Philipsburg are on or near Front Street, it can get very crowded if there are cruise ships in the harbor. Marigot has shops in several locations and far fewer passengers shop there.

Shopping Tips

⊚ Shops in Sint Maarten accept payment in florins and dollars. Those in Saint Martin accept payment in francs and dollars. Florins are not accepted in French Saint Martin, nor are francs accepted in Dutch Sint Maarten. Your best bet is to pay with dollars. Major credit cards and traveler's checks are accepted in shops but not at the market.

- ◎ Salespeople do speak English but those in Saint Martin are often less fluent.

- ◎ The island is a duty-free port. Prices average 25% less than in the U.S.

★ DID YOU KNOW?

Guavaberry liqueur, formerly made at home, is now sold in island shops. Guavaberries (not guavas) are indigenous to St. Martin.

Shopping Hours

Shopping hours vary but generally shops in Philipsburg open at 9 am and close at 6 pm, Monday through Saturday. Those in Maho Village stay open till 11 pm. Shops in Saint Martin are open from 9:30 am to 12:30 pm and 3 pm till 7 pm, Monday through Saturday. Generally closed on Sunday, shops on both sides will open if several cruise ships are expected.

Customs Regulations

U.S. citizens, regardless of age, who have been out of the country for 48 hours and have not used their duty-free allowance within 30 days, are entitled to a $600 duty-free tax exemption. Families traveling together can pool their exemptions. One quart of liquor can be included in the exemption for those over 21.

Canadian citizens who have been out of the country for seven days are permitted a duty-free exemption of $500 Canadian, and $200 Canadian for those out of the country for 48 hours. Exemptions may not be pooled.

Philipsburg

Front Street & Old Street

Front Street, running parallel to the harbor, is lined with shops on both sides. Old Street, at the eastern end of Front Street, is gated and closed to traffic. It has very nice shops.

H. Stern Jewelers. The highly regarded international jeweler specializes in 18K gold jewelry and colorful Brazilian gems such as aquamarines and tourmalines. Watches include the H. Stern sapphire collection, Concord, Esquire and Krieger Chronometers.

Little Switzerland. A "department store" that has mini-boutiques selling fine china, crystal, figurines, fragrances and leather. It is the exclusive distributor of Rolex and also sells Omega, Cartier and Raymond Weil. Rosenthal, Wedgewood, Orrefors and Lladro are among the specialties. Also sells apparel and has a Nicole Miller boutique.

Also in Marigot.

Ashburry's. Prima Classe and Pierre Balmain leathers, Porsche sunglasses, skin care products such as La Prairie and Orlane, luggage and fragrances are sold in this very attractive shop.

Also in Marigot.

New Amsterdam. A potpourri of cigars, including Cohibas, Partagas and Montecristos. Nautica and Polo shops and linens.

Dalila. Indonesian Batik cloth in original designs made into cruisewear, including pareos. Wood carvings and wall hangings too.

Old Street & Marigot.

Shipwreck Shop. Caribbean handicrafts including wood carvings, baskets, island spices, jellies and cookbooks.

Also in Marigot.

Beach Stuff. Sells exactly that. Name brand beach and resortwear. Original t-shirts, dock shoes and accessories. Names like Oakley, Baja Blues and Jams, among others.

Old Street and also in Marigot.

Rams, Maneks and Kohinoor. The three largest shops that specialize in electronics and cameras. You'll find Aiwa, Sony, Panasonic, Bose, Nikon, Minolta and Pentax among other well-known brands. Stock and price varies from shop to shop.

Also in Marigot.

Dutch Delfts Blue Gallery. Sells the handpainted Dutch porcelain in the traditional blue and white design as well as the newer Imari line, which has roots in ancient Japan. All

Old Street.

items are imported and come with a certificate of authenticity.

Also in Marigot.

Lipstick. All the most popular fragrances, cosmetics and skin care products, including Shiseido, Boucheron, Oscar de la Renta and scores of others.

Also in Marigot.

Goldfinger. A large jeweler that also stocks fine watches, such as Movado, Piaget, Corum, Esquire and Concord.

Old Street.

Barrel. Sells imported liquors and wines. Good buys.

Blackswan Boutique. Sells beachwear, including Gottex bathing suits.

Gold Mine. The exclusive agent for Tiffany jewelry and gifts. Fine watches, including Hublot, Carrera and Carrera, Patek Philippe and Breitling Chronomats.

America West India company. Sells island crafts and prints.

St. Maarten Guavaberry company. Sells the island's guavaberry liqueur and other island crafts.

Tommy Hilfinger. A boutique that sells clothing designed by Hilfinger.

Marigot

Marigot shops are near the **Port La Royale Marina** and on **Rue de la République, Rue de la Liberté** and **Rue Charles de Gaulle**. Many more shops here sell designer clothing and accessories. Some shops are branches of Philipsburg stores.

Oro del Sol. A beautifully designed shop with several boutiques. The main shop sells jewelry, including Hublot, Mikimoto, Bulgari and Ebel. The Cartier Boutique sells the famed watches and gift items. A third boutique has extensive collections of Baccarat and Lalique crystal, Christofle silverware and Villeroy and Boch china. Still another sells Mont Blanc pens and leather desk sets and daily organizers.

République and Liberté.

European Jewelers. Authentic Italian gold and stone jewelry that is specifically hand-crafted for the shop as well as famous Swiss timepieces by Cyma, Tabbah and Jean Lasalle.

Rue Général de Gaulle.

La Romana. Ladies' fashions, including lingerie and swimwear and leathers from Fendi and Moschino.

République.

Colombian Emeralds. Specializes in gold jewelry and particularly items set with emeralds. A new line of jewelry called "Sea Treasures" is moderate in price. Fine watches too.

République.

Liberté.

La Casa del Habano. A shop that sells fine cigars, most imported from Cuba but also from the Dominican Republic and Jamaica.

Marina.

Italmania. A boutique selling ladies' clothing imported from Italy.

Marina.

Gingerbread and Mahogany. An art gallery that specializes in Haitian art. Original paintings and prints. Tapestries.

Howell Center.

Match. A supermarket that sells pâtés, cheeses and other foods imported from France. Great for picnics.

Rue Général de Gaulle.

Papagayo. A delightful shop that sells Caribbean handicrafts, including woodcarvings, watercolors, straw items and gifts.

La Goût du Vin (Rue de Anguilla, near the Post Office). Sells imported French wines and champagnes.

Rive Gauche. A boutique that sells Mondi silks, Moschino leathers and designer sunglasses.

Marina.

Havane. Armani and Versace clothing.

Rue Général de Gaulle.

Act III and Jet Set. Attractive boutiques that sell French and Italian (and U.S.) clothing and resortwear for men and women. Escada, Cerruti Jeans and La Coste are represented.

Rue Général de Gaulle

Beauty & Scents. Fragrances and cosmetics and skincare products. Also a beauty salon.

Banana Market Place. A small plaza near the library that sells locally made jewelry using black pearls, handmade clothing, rums and spices.

Marina L'Epicerie. A French delicatessen that sells caviar, smoked salmon, pâtés and Kedieard Petrossian products.

Maho Village

There is a small shopping center here. Shops stay open until 11 pm and are often open Sundays. Some are branch stores of shops on Front Street.

Jewelry Stores. Colombian Emeralds, Gold Factory, JN Jewelers, Jewels & Linens.

Island Handicrafts. Arts & Crafts, Shipwreck Shop, Beach Stuff, Beach Bum, Out Island Trader.

Fragrances. Sparky's, Maho Clinic.

Clothing. Lacoste, Dalila, Benetton, Angelique.

Art Galleries

French Side

Roland Richardson. Galleries in Marigot (dock) and Orleans. ☎ 590-87-32-24. A painter and native son has become a chronicler of the island's sites, traditions and people.

Minquet Gallery. Rambaud Hill (between Marigot and Grand Case), ☎ 590-87-76-06. Born in France but a long-time island resident, Minquet has won awards for paintings of the island's flora and its sites.

Dona Bryhiel Gallery. Les Alizes, Oyster Pond. ☎ 590-87-43-93. Born in Marseille, the artist has had exhibits worldwide for her richly colored paintings of island life.

Other galleries include: **Graffitti**, with galleries in Marigot (Liberte) and on Blvd. Grand Case; **Galerie 105** and **Lynn Studio** are neighbors on Blvd. Grand Case.

Dutch Side

Greenwith Gallery. Front Street, ☎ 599-5-23842. Sells watercolors and lithographs about the island in "primitive" style.

Simpson Bay Art Gallery. Airport Road, ☎ 599-5-43464. Has a large selection of paintings, lithographs and prints by local artists.

Best Places to Stay

An early decision you'll have to make is whether to stay in Dutch Sint Maarten or in French Saint Martin. Keep in mind that distances are short, so you can easily stay on the Dutch side and dine in Marigot or Grand Case or stay on the French side and spend the evening winning the jackpot at a casino in Maho Bay. Where to stay is more a matter of the type of hotel you like than its location.

Generally, hotels on the Dutch side are highrise resorts or large villa communities that can accommodate hundreds of guests (Maho Bay Beach Hotel has 600 guest rooms). They would be at home in Miami, although they are individually located and not on one strip. The decor is contemporary, without traditional Caribbean architecture or furnishings. Instead you will find satellite TVs, in-room safes, stocked minibars, several restaurants, shops and on-property casinos. There are a few guest houses and inns and a growing number of developments that involve time-sharing options. While there is no hard sell, you will be reminded of this by the sales desks.

Established French-side hotels are in low-rise buildings – often two-story attached buildings set in landscaped grounds. Painted in pastel colors with peaked roofs and traditional gingerbread trim, they have wicker and rattan furnishings and private patios or terraces. They normally have kitchenettes. Even the cluster of moderately priced hotels recently built on Nettle Bay are in this traditional style, although they are larger and some accommodate over 100 guests, a rarity on the French side. There are villa communities here, many of them near Orient Bay, but no time-sharing.

Hotels on both sides of the island have English-speaking staff.

📖 **TIP**

You should inquire about special air/hotel packages and be aware that rates in high season are as much as 30% more than off-season. Also note that a few hotels on the French side close for a time in the summer to allow for refurbishing and for staff vacations.

Villa Rentals

There are many more hotel rooms available on St. Martin, so villa rentals are not as popular as they are on St. Barts, where rooms are limited. However, there are individually owned villas

and condos that can be rented by those who prefer the seclusion these accommodations offer.

Rental Agencies

ON THE ISLAND

Cariono, Rue du Général de Gaulle,
Marigot, ☎ 590-87-57-58; fax 590-87-71-88.

Immobilier St. Martin Caraïbes, Rue du
Général de Gaulle, Marigot, ☎ 590-87-
55-21; fax 590-87-81-93.

IN THE U.S.

WIMCO, Newport, RI, ☎ 800-932-3222.

Villas of Distinction, Armonk, NY,
☎ 800-289-0900.

🔲 TIP

Hotels on the Dutch side add a
5% tax to all hotel bills and a
10% to 15% service charge as
well. French side hotels add a
taxe de séjour (visitor's tax) to
hotel bills. Although it varies
from hotel to hotel, it is often
5% per person. They also add a
10% to 15% service charge.

Hotels accept major credit cards, although a
few small spots require a cash (check) deposit
when making reservations.

Alive Price Scale

The scale below is based on 1998 prices for a double room in high season without taxes or surcharges. It is designed to give you a heads-up about hotel rates so you can select a stop within your budget, but always call and check.

Deluxe . . . . Over $300

Expensive $225-300

Moderate $150-225

Inexpensive . . . . under $150

Seasonal Concerns

High season is November 15 through April 15. Off-season rates are as much as 30% less, and there are special packages available year-round.

The Best Hotels on Saint Martin

La Samanna

Closed Sept. & Oct.

B.P. 4077, Baie Lounge
St. Martin, FWI 97064
☎ 590-87-64-00; fax 590-87-87-86
Deluxe

Management of this deluxe resort has been in
the capable hands of the Orient Express Hotel
Group since 1996. Badly damaged by Hurricane Luis, La Samanna was closed for several
months and was tastefully renovated and refurbished by Rosewood, the previous management
group. Few additional changes have been made
and that is just fine since the hotel is exceptional.

Set on 55 acres of beachfront on Baie Longue
(Long Bay), one of St. Martin's loveliest
beaches, and surrounded by beautiful
landscaping and gardens, are 15 Mediterranean-style villas that house suites – from junior
to three-bedroom. The whitewashed villas have
private terraces and patios. Interior curved
archways and high ceilings allow the sunlight
to brighten each room. Whatever your selection, you'll find comfortable wicker and rattan
furnishings and colorful island art and accessories. The king-sized bed will be covered in apricot and teal blue to match the pillows on the
couch and chairs. Fresh flowers and bowls of
tropical fruits will appear each day. Not identi-
cally furnished, some villas have kitchenettes,
and all have stocked mini-bars and air-
conditioning. While most villas face the beach,
there are two near the main building that are
on the hillside.

La Samanna Restaurant, on a terrace in the
main building, is one of the island's best French
restaurants (see *Dining*) and the less formal
Poolside Grill serves French and Creole dishes

at lunch (noon-5 pm) and dinner (7 pm-11 pm). Local bands often play at meals. Buffet breakfast, included in your rate, may be eaten in the restaurant or on your terrace. There is 24-hour room service.

With such a long beachstrip you might expect an active watersports program. You won't be disappointed. You can snorkel, windsurf, waterski, or sail on Long Bay and the concierge can arrange scuba or fishing trips. There are lounge chairs and thatched umbrellas along the beach and others around the angular pool. There are three tennis courts and a well-equipped gym, and you can arrange for a massage or a beauty treatment.

Over the years many international celebrities have been guests at La Samanna. They come not to "be seen," but for the privacy offered them. You'll appreciate the same.

Le Privilège Resort and Spa
Anse Marcel
St. Martin, FWI 97150
☎ 590-87-38-38; fax 590-87-44-12
Expensive

Sharing Marcel Cove with Le Meridien, Le Privilège Resort and Spa sits on the hillside overlooking the larger hotel and the bay. An unusual stop on the island, Le Privilège is a member of the "Small Luxury Hotels of the World" organization and it fits right in. Its 40 rooms and suites are set in two-story pink stucco buildings that have typical gingerbread trim. The hotel, opened in 1992, was destroyed by Hurricane Luis and had to be rebuilt. Rooms are large and elegantly furnished with rattans and island woods and floral accessories. They have tile floors, marble bathrooms, in-room safes and CD players. Some have king-sized beds. Rooms on the lower levels have patios, while the suites have terraces with ocean views. The Marina Suites have two bedrooms. A continental breakfast of fresh fruit, hot croissants and beverages can be served on your terrace or patio.

Hotel facilities include two pools, six tennis courts, four squash and two racquetball courts as well as a staffed gym. Aerobic and stretching classes are given daily.

The Health Spa Center has professionals proficient in massage, shiatsu, anti-cellulite treatment, seaweed body masks and lymphatic drainage. There is a steamroom, water jet bathtubs and a beauty salon.

There is a French restaurant and a poolside grill as well as two bars.

Le Meridien
BP 581, Anse Marcel
St. Martin, FWI 97056
☎ 590-87-67-00; fax 590-87-30-38
Expensive

On the island's northeastern shore, Marcel Cove, with a wide half-mile-long beach, is home to several hotels. The largest is Le Meridien, which is like a small village. The entrance to the cove is down a steep hill that has a guarded entrance. From atop the hill, you'll see lots of red and yellow peaked rooftops and a busy marina. These are the two- and three-story buildings that house almost 400 rooms.

The original buildings in L'Habitation, are in typical Creole style with gingerbread trim and open terraces. They contain 250 rooms. They are small but attractively furnished with colorful fabrics, area rugs and marble baths. The newer buildings, in Le Domaine, seem more contemporary in design but have antique-style furniture, lots of island ceramics and curtained baths. The Marina Suites have full kitchens. All the rooms are air-conditioned and have fans, mini-bars and refrigerators.

All have private patios or terraces, but surprisingly few of them have ocean views.

Each area has a large swimming pool, jacuzzi and sundeck, but it is the beach strip that is exceptional. The bay is busy with snorkelers, paddleboats, canoes, sunfloats, jetskis and windsurfers. The waterfront staff is very helpful. Other facilities include six tennis courts, four squash courts, two racquetball courts, an archery target and a gym. Guests here get special rates at the Privilège Spa nearby.

The main building, centrally located, looks like a plantation house. It is quite large, all marble and has marble staircases leading to the mezzanine level. The lobby has comfortable sofas and chairs, shops and a concierge.

The resort has four restaurants plus several bars. La Belle France is the upscale French restaurant. La Veranda serves Italian food and Le Barbecue serves salads, sandwiches and the like. Head to Le Balaou for a buffet breakfast. Local bands often play at night and at special theme dinners.

◫ TIP

Le Meridien is most popular with French guests and you'll find fewer English-speaking people here.

La Belle Créole Hotel
Pointe du Bluff, Nettle Bay
St. Martin, FWI 97965
☎ 590-87-66-00; fax 590-87-56-66
Expensive

One of the last hotels to reopen after being devastated by Hurricane Luis, La Belle Créole welcomed guests again in late fall 1997. Poised at the tip of a 25-acre peninsula that juts into Nettle Bay, its location is both its glory and its predicament. It has unobstructed views of Marigot and Fort Louis, but there were no mountains to shield it from the high winds. It is a deluxe stop (even if the buildings are painted in lipstick pink). Its 166 air-conditioned rooms and suites are housed in stucco buildings designed to recreate an elegant Mediterranean fishing village complete with cobblestone courtyards. The "village" sits on two sandy strips and has palm trees and all new landscaping. All accommodations have informal furnishings, TVs and minibars. Those without balconies have large picture windows. The resort has a good size pool and jacuzzi, a fitness center and tennis courts. There is an outdoor café as well as a fine French-Creole restaurant.

The beachfront watersports center has a wide range of equipment. The entrance to La Belle Créole is through a gated drive off Bay Nettle - Sandy Ground Road.

L'Esplanade Caraïbes Hotel
Grand Case
St. Martin, FWI 97150
☎ 590-87-06-55; fax 590-87-29-15
Moderate/Expensive

A personal favorite, L'Esplanade is small and its architecture is not the typical Creole design. Eyecatching, it sits on a hillside not far from the town of Grand Case. Only a half-dozen years old, it is beautifully maintained and spotless. The staff is always dusting, polishing and especially gardening. A magnificent rock garden filled with colorful tropical flowers surrounds the sundeck and pool area.

The hotel has 24 rooms in parallel two-story Mediterranean-style buildings. The central courtyard serves as the reception area. Accommodations include studios and suites, some with loft bedrooms and some duplexes. They have king-sized beds, cathedral ceilings and mahogany staircases to the sleeping or office alcoves. There are sleeper sofas in the living rooms. Furnishings are contemporary and terraces front each suite. Each has a satellite TV, in-room safe and modern bath.

Stone staircases lead from the lobby level to the pool and sundeck. No beach or restaurant, but the beach and scores of restaurants are just minutes away, even on foot.

Grand Case Beach Club
Grand Case
St. Martin, FWI 97150
☎ 590-87-51-87; fax 590-87-59-93
Moderate

Closed Sept.

With its lovely location on a secluded cove adjacent to Grand Case Village and its friendly American management, the Beach Club was sorely missed by its loyal clientele in the aftermath of Hurricane Luis. It took a year for renovations and refurbishing to be completed, but the results were worth the wait. It's rather like a new hotel. Your choices include 72 studios and 15 one- or two-bedroom suites in a series of teal and white low-rise buildings. Three of the buildings are on Grand Case Beach and another is on the Club's second beach, Petit Plage, where a new restaurant, boutique and watersports center are now located. Suites have kitchens and some studios have sleeping lofts. All rooms have air-conditioning, satellite TVs and private terraces fronted by sliding glass doors. There is a pool and tennis court. Continental breakfast can be served in your room. A new bar area has bloomed where Café Panoramique once reigned. The new restaurant serves pasta and burgers. Ask for an ocean view. The mysterious shape on the horizon is Anguilla.

Little Key Beach Hotel
Cul de Sac
St. Martin, FWI 97150
☎ 590-87-49-19; fax 590-87-49-23
Expensive

On a secluded bay, Little Key Beach Hotel was completed in 1997. It was the site of the Golden Tulip Hotel, but the owners decided not to rebuild when the hotel was destroyed by Hurricane Luis. This is a deluxe resort with a very modern main building. There are only 94 spacious units and each is air-conditioned, and has a refrigerator and a large terrace. Furnishings are Creole with wicker, rattan and florals predominating. There are three pools, a terrace restaurant and bar, a health club and gym, and an activity program. A watersports center sits on the beach at the base of the hillside. Ferries from this beach go to uninhabited Lilet Pinel, where there is excellent snorkeling.

Mississippi
Oyster Pond
Saint Martin, FWI 97150
☎ 590-87-33-81; fax 590-87-31-52
Moderate-Expensive

Not your typical Creole hotel, Mississippi is not painted in pastel shades but instead uses glossy woods on its terraces and walls and in its lobby. It really stands out.

The hotel is very small, with only 13 one- or two-bedroom suites in attached two-level buildings topped by green peaked roofs with gingerbread trim and carved terraces. The suites are large and have king-sized beds, rattan sofas and chairs with floral pillows and drapes, TVs, VCRs and stereo systems. There is a stocked mini-bar, a refrigerator and microwave and air-conditioning. The bathrooms, of pink Portuguese marble, have oversized bathtubs with jacuzzis. Each suite has a terrace that faces the pool and sea.

The lobby is small but very attractive, with a gleaming wood reception desk, wicker furniture and track lights. The pool is just a few steps away and it is long enough for lap swimming. Lounge chairs of dark wood are covered by dark blue pads and the same wood is on the beach umbrellas and adjacent bar and restaurant. Le Mahogany is quite elegant at night when it serves grilled meats, salads and Creole dishes.

The hotel is near the marina but a long walk away from a beach; Taking a car is the best option.

Hotel Beach Plaza
Baie de Marigot
Saint Martin, FWI 97150
☎ 590-87-87-00; fax 590-87-18-87
Moderate

Totally refurbished in 1996, the Beach Plaza is not an elegant stop but it does have a lot to offer. It is on Sandy Ground Road, just a five-minute walk to Marigot and it has a small sandy beach on Marigot Bay where you can tan, swim or enjoy a pedal boat. The hotel's major asset is its long freshwater pool and sundeck.

All the hotel's public rooms are off the pink tiled lobby that is glass-topped and has plants and ponds that lend a greenhouse effect. The piano bar and restaurant are here, along with shops and car rental agencies. The glass roof lets the sunlight keep the hotel bright.

The 154 rooms (including some suites and deluxe studios) are on the three upper floors. Open terraces allow the rooms to be visible from the lobby level. Rooms have floral bedspreads and drapes, light wood furniture, air-conditioners, refrigerators and small satellite TVs.

Terraces front every room. They face the sea or the marina.

Captain Oliver's Resort
Oyster Pond
Saint Martin, FWI 97150
☎ 590-87-40-26; fax 590-87-40-84
Moderate-Expensive
Captain Oliver's Resort is one of the island's most popular hideaways and deservedly so. Its terrific location, attractive rooms, excellent restaurant and active marina are all pluses, but it's an intangible, perhaps its Gallic charm, that makes it so alluring. There is a Captain Oliver and his resort has straddled the French-Dutch border for almost 20 years. The hotel's 50 junior suites are in the French West Indies, while the restaurant is built on a jetty over the horseshoe shaped bay, which is in Dutch waters.

In an attempt to make the resort look like a ship, wood plank bridges with rope handrails lead from the comfortable lobby to the hotel area and to the restaurant. The suites, with ocean or marina views, are large, light and airy. White is the predominant color on the walls, tile floors, bamboo furniture and peaked beamed ceilings. Colorful floral bedcovers and drapes add an island touch. Each suite has a private terrace where you can enjoy breakfast, included in the rate. Air-conditioned, they have king-sized or twin beds, mini-bars and kitchenettes and satellite TV.

The restaurant (see *Dining*) specializes in Creole dishes, particularly seafood. The hotel offers shuttle service to nearby beaches. The marina (see *Sunup to Sundown*) has shops, including a grocery.

Alizea
Mont Vernon
St. Martin, FWI 97150
☎ 590-87-33-42; fax 590-87-41-15
Moderate

The name Alizea was taken from Les Alizes, the trade winds that cool these islands and blow gently across the terraces of this hilltop hotel. Surrounded by lush tropical plants and flowers, Alixea has a stunning view of Orient Bay, but it's removed from the beach's frenetic pace. Because it is small, guests get to know one another and the friendly owners make everyone feel right at home.

Each of the 18 studios and the eight one-bedroom bungalows are tastefully decorated with small touches that give each its own style. You'll find wickers, carved headboards, wood-beamed ceilings with fans and colorful wall hangings. Every room has a kitchenette and an oversized terrace. The Alizea restaurant (see *Dining*) is one of the island's best. It serves French, Creole and Vietnamese food. The Alizea has a pool and there is a path to the beach. It's a 15-minute walk.

La Plantation

Orient Bay
Saint Martin, FWI 97150
☎ 590-29-58-00; fax 590-29-58-08
Moderate-Expensive

La Plantation's location, set back just a few feet from the bustling restaurants and watersports centers of Orient Beach, may not be your cup of tea if you're looking for peace and quiet. The action starts early and goes on well into the night. The inn, surrounded by banana trees, consists of a series of Colonial-style villas all on one level and all with two studios and one suite. It looks like a Creole motel with pastel walls and white verandas, but the suites are surprisingly attractive. They are decorated in pastel-colored rattan furniture with comfortable cushions you can really sink into. They are air-conditioned, have modern kitchens and baths, satellite TVs and in-room safes. The inn has a swimming pool, although most guests head to the nearby beach. Continental breakfast included.

Mont Vernon Hotel

Box 1174 Orient Bay
St. Martin, FWI 97062
☎ 590-87-62-00; fax 590-87-37-27
Moderate-Expensive

On an exposed bluff high above Orient Bay, Mont Vernon was a prime target for Hurricane Luis. Badly damaged, the hotel closed to rebuild, redecorate and relandscape. A lot of francs were spent and the upgrades are highly visible. The hotel sprawls across the hilltop, with its main pastel building at the core and a score of tri-level attached buildings around it. Named for Caribbean islands, those that face the ocean – Guadeloupe, Aruba and Antigua – have great views. Mont Vernon is an all-suite hotel that has 338 junior suites and 32 Atlantic suites. These are larger and have two bedrooms. All the suites are good size, have rattan and wicker furniture, refrigerators and TVs. All are air-conditioned and have private terraces covered by gingerbread rooftops.

A beehive of activity, the hotel has a large swimming pool and sundeck, tennis courts, ping pong tables, dart boards and a fitness center. It's a short stroll to the beach where sand volleyball games draw lots of players and lots of kibitzers and where the watersports center has all kinds of gear to rent.

The lobby is large but often filled with tour groups. Lunch is served at The Sloop at poolside, while a buffet breakfast and dinner are served at La Créole in the main building.

Hotel Anse Margot
Baie Nettle
St. Martin, FWI 97150
☎ 590-87-92-01; fax 590-87-92-13
Moderate

Although it has 96 rooms, the Anse Margot has managed to retain a smaller, more intimate French ambience. The grounds, with lots of palm trees and flowering plants, are immaculate. The eight three-story Creole buildings are connected by brick walkways. It is their design that sets them apart. They zig-zag to create more room and each terrace or patio (every unit has one) has some privacy and an unobstructed garden or beach view. You'll find browns and corals on the sofas, barrel chairs and bedspreads and French shutter doors to the terrace. All are air-conditioned, have TVs (no satellite), VCRs, safes and refrigerators.

There are two swimming pools with jacuzzis and the attractive Entre Deux Mers restaurant is set between them. American breakfasts, drinks and dinner are served here.

◻ **TIP**

The hotel has a small beach on Simpson Lagoon where you can jet ski or windsurf.

Quieter than its neighbors, Anse Margot is a good choice.

Laguna Beach Hotel
Baie Nettle
St. Martin, FWI 97150
☎ 590-87-91-75; fax 590-87-81-65
Moderate

A smaller 60-room stop, Laguna Beach shares the French shore of Simson Lagoon with its much larger neighbors. The majority of guests here are couples, although the larger mezzanine rooms can accommodate up to two children (free until age 12). The good size suites and mezzanines, all air-conditioned, have tile floors, light woods and multi-colored sofas and chairs. They have in-room safes, satellite TVs and modern bathrooms, showers only. Each has a small balcony.

The property is nicely landscaped and there are palms and tropical flowers encircling the pool and sundeck. There are three tennis courts. Café Caraïbes, near the pool and lagoon, serves buffet breakfasts and French and Creole dishes at dinner. You can swim at the lagoon but for watersports rentals you'll have to head to one of the nearby hotels.

Le Flamboyant
Nettle Bay
St. Martin, FWI 97150
☎ 590-87-60-00; fax 590-87-99-57
Moderate

Le Flamboyant's occupancy rate is high year-round because it offers good value for the franc. Though not luxurious, its 271 suites are scattered in a score of two-story red-roofed buildings. It leaves a lot of open space that's filled by stone pathways and attractive landscaping. The comfortable lobby is adjacent to the large pool, sundeck and beachfront restaurant, La Terrasse. It serves lunch and dinner as well as buffets on theme nights.

An all-suite hotel, the junior suites can sleep three, while the larger one- and two-bedroom suites can sleep four to six people. All are air-conditioned and some have kitchenettes, often popular with families with young children. Every suite has a balcony. Those facing the lagoon are slightly more expensive.

There are two pools (one for children), tennis courts, and a fitness center. Organized activities include water aerobics, water and basket polo and beach volleyball. There is a children's playground.

The Flamboyant has a 1,200-foot stretch of beach on Simpson Lagoon (across the water is Dutch St. Maarten) where you can windsurf, paddle a kayak or just swim.

▣ TIP

If you like your water with waves, there's a shuttle service to nearby Baie Rouge, a stunning beach.

Marine Hotel Simson Beach

BP 172 Nettle Bay
St. Martin, FWI 97150
☎ 590-87-54-54; fax 590-87-92-11
Moderate

Another of the hotels along the Baie Nettle strip, the Marine draws many European guests who like the moderate price and the family oriented atmosphere. The large lobby, with blue wicker sofas and chairs and bright yellow floral pillows, is often crowded with guests and children. Accommodations are in three-story attached buildings surrounded by tropical plants and trees. There are 120 studios that can sleep two adults and one child and 45 one-bedroom suites that can sleep two adults and two children. Air-conditioned with kitchenettes, each has a terrace facing the beach or the garden. Lowest floors have patios.

Days here begin with a large buffet breakfast served at the poolside LaViBo Kaye Restaurant. There is also a children's pool. Families wile away the day at the beach on the lagoon. The watersports center has pedal boats, sea scooters, jet skis and snorkel gear. There are tennis courts, ping pong tables, volleyball courts and pétanque (the French equivalent of bocce). The staff organizes activities for adults and children. The restaurant often has theme nights.

Blue Beach Hotel

26 Oyster Pond
St. Martin, FWI 97150
☎ 590-87-33-44; fax 590-87-42-13
Moderate

Nestled on the hillside near Oyster Pond Bay overlooking the Atlantic and the Oyster Pond Marina, the 19 rooms and suites in the red-roofed Creole-style bungalows are comfortable but without any frills. Air-conditioned, each has a kitchenette and private terrace. There is a large pool and sundeck, and a poolside restaurant called Frogs that serves French and Creole food. Many guests at Blue Beach are scuba divers, sailors or fishermen involved in programs at the marina.

Pavillon Beach Hotel

BP 313 Grand Case
St. Martin, FWI 97150
☎ 590-87-96-46; fax 590-87-71-04
Moderate

At the heart of Grand Case, the Pavillon has six studios, 10 one-bedroom suites and one deluxe honeymoon suite with a king-sized bed. Decorated in warm pastels and rattan, each unit has a kitchenette, air-conditioning, an in-room safe, a TV (no satellite) and a modern bathroom, shower only. Continental breakfast is served in your room.

But best of all, every room has a terrace or patio that faces the sea. Ground-floor patios open right onto the sand. A nondescript choice with a good location.

Hevea

163 Blvd. Grand Case
St. Martin, FWI 97150
☎ 590-87-56-85; fax 590-87-83-88
Moderate

The Hevea name is most associated with the gourmet French restaurant that occupies the front rooms of this restored Creole mansion. The eight-room inn, owned by the same family, is marked by the awning-covered walkway. The rooms are tiny like so many on Paris' Left Bank, but each is distinctive. They have wood-beamed ceilings and carved mahogany headboards and dressers. There are colorful wall-hangings and ceramic pieces in each room. Bathrooms are modern and a small patio or terrace fronts each room. The three suites have kitchenettes and there are also three studios and two double rooms. Only five are air-conditioned; the others have ceiling fans. Breakfast, included in the rate, is served in the charming Creole sitting room. The inn is across the street from Grand Case Beach and scores of restaurants are within strolling distance.

Guests get discounts on dinner at Hevea.

Hotel Atlantide

Box 5140 Grand Case
St. Martin, FWI 97150
☎ 590-87-09-80; fax 590-87-12-36
Moderate

Fronting Grand Case Boulevard, the Atlantide looks out of place. It is a modern building with none of the French-Creole architecture that makes other stops here so attractive. So it was a pleasant surprise to find 10 bright and airy studios and suites with terraces that look out on Grand Case Beach. Studios have a double bed and a small sitting area. Suites have one or two bedrooms. They have light pastel walls and floral or striped furnishings. Kitchenettes have dining bars. You can also eat on the terrace, which has folding wood doors to keep out the light. The hotel has lounge chairs and umbrellas on the beach.

Hotel Marina Royale
Rue St. James, Marigot
St. Martin, FWI 97150
☎ 590-87-52-46; fax 590-87-92-88
Inexpensive

You can't ask for a better location if you are here on business. Right in the heart of Marigot, on the marina and surrounded by shops and restaurants, the Marina Royale is your best bet in Marigot proper. It has 70 units – most are studios but a few are larger suites. All have terraces, kitchenettes, air-conditioners and satellite TVs. While the hotel was largely untouched by the hurricane, its pool was totally destroyed. Rebuilt, it will cool you off after a long business session. A five-minute walk will get you to the Sandy Ground Beach.

Inexpensive.

There are two other acceptable choices in Marigot. **Le Royale Louisiana** on Rue Charles de Gaulle (☎ 590-87-86-51) and **La Résidence**, also on Rue Charles de Gaulle (☎ 590-87-70-37). Rather basic, they are built around inner courtyards that have restaurants.

Morning Star Guest House
Grand Case
Saint Martin, FWI 97150
☎ 590-87-93-85; fax 590-87-72-08
Inexpensive

A family-run guest house on the main road just before the town, Morning Star has nine rooms. Each is air-conditioned and has a fully-equipped kitchenette and daily maid service. No frills but friendly owners and staff. You can walk to the beach and the restaurants in town in five minutes.

A Clothing-Optional Resort

Club Orient Naturist Resort
Orient Bay
St. Martin, FWI 97150
☎ 590-87-33-85; fax 590-87-33-76
Expensive-Moderate

In the film *A Shot in the Dark,* Inspector Clouseau pursues a murder suspect into a resort unaware that it is strictly a nudist camp. Hilarity follows. Club Orient is clothing-optional, but we opted to keep ours on while looking through. The club, badly damaged by Hurricane Luis and closed for more than one year, has been rebuilt and even enlarged. But the 47 waterfront beach chalets that had formerly been built in red pine imported from Finland are now concrete. They are safer but not as attractive, although they have retained the size and design. The studios and suites have been rebuilt in pine because they are not as exposed to the elements. Also rebuilt, the Papagayo Restaurant that looks even more attractive. Once again there is a watersports center, grocery and boutique. The club is activity-oriented and lots of activities are planned for daytime and for evenings.

Villa Communities

Green Cay Village
Box 3006 Orient Bay
St. Martin, FWI 97064
☎ 590-87-38-63; fax 590-87-39-27
Expensive
The most upscale of the villa communities at Orient Bay, Green Cay Village is set back from the beach itself on a nearby hillside. There are 16 clustered villas that hold 48 accommodations with one to three bedrooms. Each cluster has its own pool and sundeck with lounge chairs. The three-bedroom villas have two bedrooms with king-sized beds and a third with a double bed.

Painted in soft pastels with a gingerbread trim, they are quite modern inside with tile floors small area rugs, cable TVs and comfortable wicker furniture. Kitchens are fully equipped with all major appliances as well as a blender, a microwave, a barbecue grill and a coffeemaker. A first night "starter kit" of food is a nice touch. Views from the living room terrace include the beach and St. Barts.

◙ **TIP**

Green Cay guests have special rates at the rental shops and restaurants on Orient Bay. They can charge to their room.

Nettle Bay Beach Club

BP 4081, Nettle Bay
St. Martin, FWI 97064
☎ 590-87-68-68; fax 590-87-68-05
Moderate-Expensive

Centrally located between Marigot and Maho Bay, Nettle Bay Beach Club is a good choice if you like the privacy of villa living but want hotel amenities. Attractive with gray wood exteriors and white shutters and trim on the peaked rooftops, the attached beach villas are set in three large horseshoe-shaped clusters with the open end facing the sea. Each cluster has its own pool and sundeck complete with lounge chairs. Others are on the beach just a few steps away. The ground level of each villa has one or two bedrooms and a kitchenette. The walls are painted in pastels. There are tiled floors and contemporary rattan furnishings in the living room. Each veranda faces the pool and sea. On the second level, the villa studios have queen-sized beds and small sundecks. There are 200 villa accommodations.

The fourth cluster is a seven-building semi-circle called The Gardens. Each garden building has five units, smaller and less expensive than the villas. Lower level suites have king-sized beds and small sitting areas. Upper level rooms have queen-sized beds. Both have kitchenettes. An attractive garden area and pool are in the central courtyard.

There are three tennis courts on property and a watersports center nearby that offers Nettle Bay guests special rates.

Le Grand Bleu, the beachside restaurant, shares the local dining scene with La Parilla, which serves Argentine-style grilled meats, and the French and Creole La Fayette.

Esmeralda Resort
Box 5141, Orient Bay
St. Martin, FWI 97071
☎ 590-87-36-36; fax 590-87-35-18
Moderate-Expensive
Although it looks like a suburban housing development, Esmeralda is actually an attractive villa community that operates as a hotel. Fifteen villas, comprised of 54 rooms and suites, offer all the comforts of a home and the amenities of a resort. Each of the villa clusters has its own swimming pool and jacuzzi. Functionally decorated with rust tile floors, pale yellow walls and colorful florals on the sofas, chairs and coverlets, it is designed for families. The suites, with two to five bedrooms, have fully equipped kitchens and king, queen and twin beds. Rooms and suites can be joined to form larger units. There is daily maid service, satellite TV and a concierge to offer sightseeing trips and arrange for babysitting if necessary.

Esmeralda has a small beach with a water-sports center and it is just a short walk to Orient Beach and its restaurants. There are two lighted tennis courts and a good on-property restaurant, L'Astrolobe. You can enjoy breakfast and dinner (French) here.

The Best Hotels on
Sint Maarten

Oyster Bay Beach Resort
Box 239
St. Maarten, Netherlands Antilles
☎ 599-5-22206; fax 599-52-5695
Expensive

Heading east from Princess Juliana Airport and Philipsburg, you'll pass the Old Salt Pond that made St. Maarten so important to the Dutch and West Indies communities with great names such as Sucker Garden and Naked Boy Hill. Soon you'll see the turnoff for Dawn Beach and Oyster Pond. Narrow and potholed, it's not what you'd expect. But, at the top of yet another rise, a mirage appears. It's on the Dutch side of Oyster Pond but looks like something from French Morocco. A whitewashed building with Moorish arches and two stone towers is set on a promontory surrounded by green hills and calm blue waters. It's the Oyster Bay Beach Resort, a small 40-room gem. The lobby, with sturdy white wicker sofas, rocking chairs and tables, is between the towers and an open courtyard is just beyond it. The courtyard has a bar and umbrella-covered tables and the candlelit gourmet French restaurant.

The original 20 rooms (built when the hotel was the Oyster Pond Beach Hotel) are in the main building. Six are on the ground level and the others on the second floor around a white walkway with dark wooden balustrades. Named for famous old sailing ships, they have patios or terraces and a few are duplex. The newer Ocean Suites sit along the narrowing bluff. They are larger and more luxuriously appointed, but the façades are not Moorish. Each air-conditioned guest room has white wicker furniture, rust tile floors, French pastel fabrics and colorful lithographs. Hairdryers, small refrigerators and bathrobes are also standard. Suites have tubs while studios have only showers.

回 TIP

The new owners plan additional suites and an expansion of the facilities, including a timeshare option. These may be operational by the time you arrive.

There is a saltwater pool set amid a rock garden. Dawn Beach is just a short stroll away. Oyster Bay Resort is planning a watersports facility there.

French gourmet food is served nightly in the courtyard restaurant on fine Rosenthal china. Continental breakfast can be served in your room.

A wonderful choice. Hopefully the new additions won't overwhelm the facilities.

Maho Beach Hotel & Casino
Maho Bay
St. Maarten, Netherlands Antilles
☎ 599-5-52115; fax 599-5-53180
Expensive

If you're going on vacation but don't want to get away from it all, the Maho Beach Hotel Complex is for you. It's not just a hotel, it's a village. The hotel itself has 600 guest rooms, 400 of which are in a newer wing. These are housed in a cluster of pink and white high-rise buildings with views of the sea, landscaped gardens and the village. Rooms are large, have cable TV and contemporary furnishings without a hint of Creole style. Some have king-sized beds. All rooms have private terraces.

✦ WARNING

One important drawback here is the runway of Princess Juliana Airport, which is adjacent to the grounds. If you like to sleep in, ask for a room in the west wing.

The facilities at Maho have to be larger than life to accommodate guests. Management has added new pools (there are now three), lots of lounge chairs both on the beach and on pool sundecks, three tennis courts, a hot tub and a well-stocked and well-staffed waterfront center. There are lots of organized activities as well. To cool off, you can have a cool drink at the swim-up bar.

The complex has 10 restaurants, including cafés, pizzerias, and gourmet continental and Italian spots. The shopping center has three sections and includes jewelers, a deli, local handicrafts and resortwear/t-shirt shops.

Adjacent to the hotel lobby, which is very large and comfortable, is the Royal Islander Club with its own 130 timeshare apartments and pool.

After dinner you can visit the on-property theater, disco or the largest casino on the island, the Casino Royale.

Not everyone's cup of tea, Maho is a unique experience – Greenwich Village on the Sea.

Great Bay Beach Hotel & Casino
Box 310, Philipsburg
Sint Maarten, Netherlands Antilles
☎ 599-5-22446; fax 599-5-23859
Expensive-Moderate
The Great Bay Beach Hotel & Casino is on a small peninsula at the western tip of Great Bay, just a 10-minute stroll from Philipsburg,

that fronts the heart of the bay. It has 285 rooms, each with a private patio or terrace. Rooms are good size, air-conditioned, have satellite TVs and contemporary furnishings with not a Creole touch in sight. However, you'll see the Creole style in the very large, plant-filled lobby, which features wicker furniture with pink pillows to match the striped awnings over the open-air arches facing Philipsburg. Many guests enjoy colorful tropical drinks here in the afternoon.

The hotel has two freshwater pools with sundecks and lounge chairs. Additional chairs are on the adjacent beach. The young staff has waterskiis, windsurfers, waverunners and sailboats, and even give pool scuba lessons. Organized activities include pool aerobics and beach volleyball, as well as a host of other games. There are ping pong tables, shuffleboard and tennis courts, and a fitness center.

The hotel has several dining options as well as beach barbecues and theme night parties. After dinner, guests head to the nightclub or casino in the hotel or those in Philipsburg. Taxis are always available at the hotel and you can find parking in town at night.

Timeshare Resorts

Timesharing is ubiquitous on Dutch Sint Maarten. The option is offered in huge resort complexes, in the tiny 14-room Mary's Boon Inn and even the luxurious Oyster Bay Resort. We have detailed only a few of the resorts that also operate as hotels.

Pelican Resort & Casino

Box 431 Simpson Bay
☎ 599-5-42503; fax 599-5-42133

It has only 342 guest rooms, half the number of nearby Maho Beach Hotel, but the Pelican Resort looks much larger because the buildings that house the junior, one- and two-bedroom suites are scattered throughout the property and not clustered. You can easily get lost within the complex. Suites have air-conditioned bedrooms, cable TV, fully equipped kitchens with all major appliances, and contemporary furnishings. The living room and dining areas are cooled by ceiling fans and by breezes that flow over the sea and in from the private terrace. Pelican has five pools, including one for kids, two long beach strips and an open-sea marina. The watersports center is well stocked with gear. There is a deli, a market, a medical office, a shopping arcade and barbecue grills. The four tennis courts can be lit for night play. There is a fitness center and a beauty salon. Restaurants include a steak and seafood house, a bistro and a café. There is a large casino.

Little Bay Beach & Racquet Club

Box 961, Philipsburg
☎ 599-5-22333; fax 599-5-23911

A deluxe choice operated by Divi Resorts, well known in Aruba and Bonaire, Little Bay is set

on the tip of the peninsula that juts out into
Great Bay. Secluded and romantic, it was so
badly damaged by Hurricane Luis that it was
closed for 1½ years and virtually rebuilt from
the ground up. The effort was well worth it.
Small, and unlike other resorts here that would
fit seamlessly into Miami Beach, Little Bay is
truly at home in the Caribbean.

Guest rooms are set in three-story attached villas with whitewashed facades, red peaked rooftops and graceful archways. They overlook the
bay or gardens. Accommodations range from
comfortable studios to three-bedroom apartments. All have Louis XV furniture, pale tiled
floors, and private patios or balconies. There
are freshwater pools, several tennis courts with
a pro, and a long beach with a watersports center. There are several on-property dining
choices and you are only a few minutes from
options in Philipsburg.

Royal Palm Beach Club
Airport Road, Simpson Bay
Sint Maarten, Netherlands Antilles
☎ 599-5-43737; fax 599-5-43727
A deluxe choice, the 140-room Royal Palm
offers only one type of accommodation – a two-
bedroom/two-bathroom suite in a modern low-
rise attached villa on Kimsha Beach near Simpson Bay. The spacious suites, decorated
attractively with rattans, wickers and floral
fabrics, can sleep six comfortably and all have
terraces that face the ocean. In-room amenities
include air-conditioning, cable TV and VCR,

fully equipped kitchen with all major appliances and a microwave and blender. There is a large pool and sundeck adjacent to the beach. It has a swim-up bar and a beachfront restaurant. There are communal picnic areas with barbecue grills, a health club and a well-stocked waterfront center. The hotel complex has a shopping arcade with a grocery store. The big surprise is that the Royal Palm does not have a good restaurant, but there are many nearby.

Millenium Beach Resort
Beacon Hill Road #2
Sint Maarten, Netherlands Antilles
☎ 599-5-54000; fax 599-5-54001
Expensive-Moderate
Set on Burgeaux Bay, near the airport and Maho Beach Village, the Millenium is a red-roofed resort on a wide promontory. It has 188 guest rooms in suites, deluxe one-bedroom suites and bungalows that can sleep six. The standard suites have contemporary furniture, are air-conditioned, and have cable TVs and mini-bars. The deluxe one-bedroom suites and bungalows have Caribbean florals and pastels, rattan and mahogany and marble bathrooms. They have fully equipped kitchens. All guest rooms have terraces. In the complex you will find three swimming pools and whirlpools, two tennis courts, a white sand beach and a good restaurant. Like a small town, it also has a small convention center and health spa.

Mary's Boon Beach Plantation
117 Simpson Bay Road
Sint Maarten, Netherlands Antilles
☎ 599-5-54235; fax 599-5-53403
Inexpensive
A legendary stop, this cozy inn has 14 large studios on the beach, south of Princess Juliana Airport and Maho Village. Each is sparsely furnished but has all the necessities, including a kitchenette, private bath and a beachfront patio. They do not have a/c, TV or phone.

The restaurant draws visitors as well as locals. The French/Creole dishes rely on the freshest ingredients so the menu is set each day. There is only one seating, at 8 pm, and you need reservations. Check the menu at that time. The restaurant is also not air-conditioned. Both the inn and the restaurant accept major credit cards.

Passangrahan Royal Guest House
15 Front Street, Box 151 Philipsburg
Sint Maarten, Netherlands Antilles
☎ 599-5-23588; fax 599-5-22885
Inexpensive
An island treasure, this 30-room Colonial inn is in the heart of Philipsburg and on the beach.

★ DID YOU KNOW?
The green and white building was formerly the governor's home and Queen Wilhelmina stayed here when she visited the island.

The oldest inn on the island.

The bar is named Sidney Greenstreet and it would not be a surprise to see Bogie and Bacall at the bar or on the wicker peacock chairs on the tiled veranda. No TV or phones in your room. There is a restaurant in addition to the bar. Inexpensive and charming.

Horny Toad Guest House
Box 30289 Simpson Bay
Sint Maarten, Netherlands Antilles
☎ 599-5-54323; fax 599-5-53316
Inexpensive

A former governor's home that has been converted into eight comfortable units, each with full equipped kitchen and a terrace that faces Simpson Bay. Rooms have recently been refurbished and while there are few frills, they certainly are comfortable. There is daily maid service.

Best Places to Eat

*F*ood glorious food, sang Oliver and his mates in the musical version of Oliver Twist. Unfortunately, they didn't have enough to eat, something that will not be your problem on this island where tourist literature boasts of over "400 tantalizing restaurants." That number may include McDonalds and greasy spoons, but there is no question that the island has a surprisingly large number of restaurants. They include elegant French bistros, brasseries, and cafés, Italian, continental, Vietnamese and American-style restaurants and a good number that serve typical Creole specialties. You can enjoy lunch and dinner overlooking a beach or on one, near a busy marina or a bustling shopping street or on the terrace of an elegant resort in a secluded cove.

The island's gastronomic center is on the French side. Marigot, which was a fishing village not so long ago, has over 50 restaurants in its "downtown." There are informal ones near the marina and port, and more formal ones in restored Creole buildings nearby. The tiny hamlet of Grand Case is not far behind with 20 superb international restaurants on its one main street. Many of these are owned and staffed by French expats, trained in the kitchens of France's finest restaurants. A bonus is that their cooking represents regional specialties from all over France.

There are no Dutch restaurants on the island, but Sint Maarten has fine international restaurants in Philipsburg and Maho, and a great many moderately priced American-style eateries as well.

Restaurants are risky businesses. A place can be "in" one year and gone the next. We have tried to select restaurants that have had staying power – some have been popular for 20 years. You'll surely find some hot new spots during your stay and we hope you'll alert us to them so that we can include them in the next edition.

回 *TIP*
Prices might be higher than you would expect. Keep in mind that everything here is imported, much of it from Europe, and the added costs are passed down. On the plus side, the prices here will still be less than you'd pay for comparable food and ambience in New York or Paris.

Dining Savvy

⊚ Make reservations for dinner, particularly in high season. Restaurants are small. In some cases reservations are *required*.

⊚ Restaurants accept major credit cards, traveler's checks and U.S. dollars. French-side restaurants accept francs and Dutch-side restaurants accept florins.

⊚ Restaurants on the French side typically serve lunch from noon to 3 pm, then close and re-open for dinner from 6:30 until 10:30 pm. Dutch-side restaurants do not close after lunch but serve all day. Many of the island's finest restaurants serve dinner only.

⊚ Unlike St. Barts, where virtually every restaurant closes for a period in the off-season, only a few French restaurants follow that trend.

⊚ Casual chic attire is the norm at the upscale dining spots. Jeans are very popular. Shorts and t-shirts are acceptable in the moderately priced eateries. Many restaurants post their menus at the door.

Alive Price Scale

Designed to give you a heads up about costs, we devised this scale based on a three-course dinner without alcoholic beverages.

Very Expensive . . . . Over $50

Expensive $35-50

Moderate $25-35

Inexpensive . . . . Under $25

🔲 TIP

Restaurants typically add a 10% to 15% service charge to the bill. It is common to leave a small additional tip for good service.

Restaurants In Or Near Marigot

Mario's Bistrot
Pont de Sandy Ground
☎ 590-87-06-36
French Nouvelle
Expensive

Just five minutes from Marigot, Mario's overlooks the canal that connects the ocean waters of Nettle Bay with the calm waters of Simpson Bay Lagoon. Our friend who winters here and another who lives here both picked Mario's as the island's best restaurant. It isn't the most elegant or even the most attractive, but the food and service are exceptional. The dining room and bar are on a roof-covered terrace with blue walls and blue tiled floors. The wood tables are near the canal so you can see the marine traffic. The menu changes frequently to take advantage of the freshest ingredients available. Some specialties include a chunky fish or vegetable soup or salmon sushi with steamed asparagus.

Look for Sandy Point Bridge.

The bouillabaisse is enough for two and among the pasta dishes the penne with cherry tomatoes stands out. The lamb chops and other meats are soft enough to cut with a fork and desserts include tarts and fresh fruits. Reservations are a must since the restaurant is small and service unhurried.

La Samanna Restaurant
Baie Longue
☎ 590-87-64-00
Classical French
Very Expensive

Everything about La Samanna Resort is understated. "When you have it, there's no need to flaunt it," could be their motto. And so it is with their gourmet French restaurant that rivals any of the independent restaurants on the island. Its setting is special as well. The restaurant is on a split level terrace in the main building that looks out over the long crescent beach. You'll dine by candlelight surrounded by the red, purple and orange aromatic flowers of the Caribbean. Reservations are a must, but come early for a pre-dinner drink and to explore the grounds. A unique, albeit expensive, hors d'oeuvre is the caviar served with blini and chilled vodka. There are three kinds of caviar to choose from. Seafood risotto or chunks of lobster with curry butter are good starters. Main courses include an unusual surf n' turf with beef tenderloins and lobster medallions in port wine and delicious tournedos of swordfish and tuna with five pepper sauce. If you like duck, it is served with raspberry sauce and fried plantains. Desserts include pastries, tarts and ice cream. Jackets are required, as are reservations. The restaurant has a wine cellar reputed to hold 20,000 bottles.

La Vie en Rose
Blvd. de France
☎ 590-87-54-42
French restaurant and café
Very Expensive

One of the first French restaurants on the island, La Vie en Rose has maintained its high standards and remains a delightful choice for a romantic dinner. On the second floor of a century-old warehouse that overlooks the harbor, the dining room is quite formal with pale pink walls and matching tablecloths. Its rattan chairs have floral cushions and antique wall sconces provide indirect lighting. Red striped awnings shade the windows on every side of the dining room and the half-dozen tables on the outer terrace which are considered choice.

Start with the smoked salmon with porcini mushrooms, salmon roe and tomatoes or the chunky lobster salad with ginger. Move on to crayfish in puff pastry or the filet of swordfish with passion fruit sauce or a mignon of lamb in venison sauce. Save room for the apple tart or chocolate mousse cake.

La Vie en Rose Café is on the first floor and has an outdoor terrace on Market Square. Here they serve sandwiches, salads and delicious pastries well into the night. The patio tables, covered by umbrellas, are especially nice.

Jean Dupont Bistro
Port Royale Marina
☎ 590-87-71-13
French/Vietnamese
Lunch and dinner
Moderate

One of the more formal restaurants around the marina, Jean Dupont has both an inner dining room and an awning-covered terrace facing the water. The fan-cooled inner room has beige rattan peacock chairs and pale tablecloths and the southeast Asian touches are reminders that the French were in Vietnam for many years. Vietnamese specialties include a delicious soup with shrimp and pineapple chunks, chicken curry and noodles with beef or chicken. Other specialties are French and include poulet chasseur (with onions and mushrooms) and boeuf bourguignon. Crêpes are among the desserts. There is a special three-course menu every night.

Le Santal By the Sea
Sandy Ground
☎ 590-87-53-48
Classic French
Dinner only
Very Expensive

Le Santal serves classic French cuisine in an attractive seaside restaurant near the Sandy Ground Bridge. It is in an unattractive residential area, but don't let the stray dogs, rusting cans and ramshackle houses dissuade you. When you cross the threshold, you'll be in a spotless white room with tables on the inner terrace. The outer one is right above the water. Sink into a brocaded chair and note the fine china and crystal and indirect lighting that gives the restaurant a warm glow.

The food is innovative and the menu changes frequently but always includes lots of salads, Norwegian salmon with chopped onion and egg, onion and asparagus soup and delicious hot and cold hors d'oeuvres. Main courses include duck with a variety of sauces, veal and lamb with red wine sauces and lobster soufflé. Crêpes Suzettes are a favorite dessert.

La Brasserie de la Gare
Port La Royale Marina
☎ 590-87-20-64
French/Italian
Open 11:30 am-10:30 pm
Inexpensive
This is the most popular restaurant at the Port La Royale, which is bustling from its 11:30 am opening till they pull the wicker chairs in at 10:30 pm. Tables are set on a roof-covered terrace and there are indoor tables as well. The inner rooms, with colorful finger paintings and TVs, are very popular with families.

回 **TIP**

The salads are enough for an entire meal and two can share one with an omelette or a sandwich.

The menu, with both French and Italian specialties, is varied enough to appeal to all appetites. There are over 20 varieties of pizza. Toppings include onions, ham, sausage, pepperoni, seafood and mushrooms.

There are lots of pasta, fish dishes, beef and chicken dishes too. You can even enjoy a cheeseburger. The Brasserie looks out onto the water and if it weren't for the 80° temperature, you'd be certain it was the Seine. Very informal.

Messalina
Blvd. de France
☎ 590-87-80-39
Northern Italian
Lunch and dinner; Closed Tuesday.
Very Expensive

Housed in a restored historical home adjoining its French sister restaurant, La Vie En Rose, Messalina finds its specialties in Northern Italy. You can start with an antipasto of cheeses, meats, marinated vegetables and cold fish which you select from a central table. This could be a perfect lunch with the crusty bread on your table. You might prefer a thick soup or a Caprese salad followed by a pasta dish. A house specialty is the lasagne, made with lobster and shrimp. Veal dishes are very popular too. Quite formal with cream-colored walls, tiled floors and light woods, it has arched doorways leading from one dining area to the other. Messalina also has tables on the terrace facing the port.

Don Camillo da Enzo

Port La Royale Marina
☎ 590-87-52-88
Italian
Dinner only, 6:30-10:30 pm
Moderate

If you prefer your Italian food in less formal surroundings, you'll enjoy Don Camillo, which is on the marina walkway. It has two dining areas. The back room has yellow walls, mauve and white tablecloths and padded wooden booths and there are tables on the outer terrace as well. Beef carpaccio, Caesar salad or mozzarella and tomatoes with olive oil are fine starters, and the meat lasagne is thick with spices. Pollo capriccosa with tomatoes and cheese and the gnocchi are delicious. Italian pastries and fruit tarts are great finishers. The popular bar here is a local meeting place. One wall displays letters and card written to the restaurant by satisfied customers from all over the world.

La Belle Epoque, ☎ 590-87-87-70, is Don Camillo's neighbor on the marina promenade. Open for lunch and dinner, it has delicious thin-crust pizzas, burgers, salads and pastas. The dinner menu adds both French and Italian dishes. As with the other restaurants on the marina, there is an inner dining area and terrace tables. Check the posted menus to see which suits your appetite best.

Le Bar de la Mer
Market Square
☎ 590-87-81-79
Eclectic Menu
Inexpensive

An island institution if you count the number of young locals wearing Le Bar's distinctive t-shirt, this place is noisy and fun to be in. The first level is virtually all bar and you have to elbow through the crowd to the second-level dining area. The menu, in French, English and Spanish, includes a dozen pizzas and they come topped with pepperoni, goat cheese, onions, anchovies, ham and peppers among other things. Burgers and club sandwiches, including a croque monsieur and a croque madame, are stuffed and look delicious. There are lots of salads and both beef and tuna tartare. Beef comes grilled as well. Most of your neighbors will be washing the food down with beer.

Le Bar's Caribbean BBQ is extremely popular. Served on the outer patio, it has grilled spiny lobsters, local snapper, huge shrimp, sirloin steaks and lamb chops, all delightfully marinated and cooked to your taste. A salad and baked potato are served with your meal. Barbecues are held nightly starting at 7 pm till the last coal dies at 11:30 pm. Reggae and calypso music in the market square is a bonus. This is a great place to meet people.

L'Arawak Café across the street is similar in style with a bar on the first level and dining on the second floor and outer patio. The menu here is more French. It too draws a young lively crowd. ☎ 590-87-99-67.

Le Charlois Grill

Rue Felix Eboue
☎ 590-87-93-19
Steakhouse
Moderate

There are times when nothing but a juicy steak will do. If that mood comes over you while you are in Marigot, head to Le Charlois, owned by a local butcher. The restaurant has high wood booths lining each wall. Each has plush velvet seats and backs. The decorations are cowhides and horns, and the Angus beef steaks and the other grilled meats are delicious. Start with an endive salad or an avocado stuffed with crabmeat. You can have beef on a brochette or lamb chops as well.

Le Marocain

Rue de Holland
☎ 590-87-83-11
Moroccan
Moderate

Like a mirage, Le Marocain rises on Holland Street, a few blocks from the waterfront. It is a beautiful restaurant with mosaic tiled floors. scalloped archways and polished wood tables inlaid with diagonals. There is even an exotic dancer on hand to entertain during dinner. Try the *mezze*, an antipasto of lots of small dishes, usually vegetables. They serve *pastelles*, pastries stuffed with meat or chicken with raisins and spices, and *tajines*, which are meat or chicken casseroles. Desserts include sweet pastries served with mint tea. Le Marocain offers an enjoyable dining experience.

La Maison Sur Le Port
At The Port
☎ 590-87-56-38
French/Creole
Lunch and dinner daily (no lunch on Sunday).
Moderate-Expensive
While other Creole buildings in Marigot have been restored, La Maison is the only one in town that still looks like a *case*, a typical creole house. You can see others in Orleans and Colombier. It is painted in a variety of pastel shades with yellow featured predominantly. It has the gingerbread trim on its long veranda and along the eaves of its colorful peaked roof. Palm trees surround the building and spraying fountains are lit at night. Two prix-fix menus are offered each day, as well as a special children's menu too. The French onion soup is exceptional and there are lots of delicious salads at lunch. Dinner has shrimp and scampi kebobs, sautéed shrimp with a crabmeat pâté, sautéed duck in passion fruit, and beef and lamb dishes as well. Crème brûlée and pastries are a fine ending.

La Brasserie de Marigot
Rue Général de Gaulle
☎ 590-87-94-43
French
Hours: 7 am to 10 pm
Inexpensive

A long block from the port, La Brasserie de Marigot has both the look and the menu of a Left Bank restaurant. It has round marble tables and wrought iron chairs in the inner dining areas and on the sidewalk. The walls are decorated with posters and paintings of Paris. It opens for breakfast at 7 am and doesn't close until 10 pm. Breakfast includes croissants, brioche and other breads served with jelly and butter. You can also order an omelette, which is served for lunch with ham, cheese, tomatoes, peppers and onions. Burgers, goat cheese and shrimp salads, and grilled fish are popular at lunch. Dinner finds hot lobster soup or gazpacho. Fish dishes include mahi mahi grilled with a vanilla or passion fruit sauce. Roast chicken, steak tartare and London broil are also dinner suggestions. Parfaits and gâteaux are among the desserts. There is a full bar.

Le Marlin

Blvd. du Front de Mer
☎ 590-87-53-38
French/Seafood
Moderate-Expensive
Closed Monday

Delicious French-style seafood and classical piano music in the background are a hard combination to beat in this small air-conditioned restaurant on the harbor walk. The inner dining room has blue and white checked tablecloths which lend a nautical look. You can also eat on the outer terrace where the salty sea air makes you even hungrier.

Starters include a hot goat cheese salad or a foie gras terrine. You can then move on to shrimp scampi, grilled lobster or a garlicky fisherman's stew. The piano man starts each night at 7 pm and switches from classical to popular to calypso as the night winds down to the 10 pm close.

Thai Garden
Sandy Ground
☎ 590-87-88-44
Thai/Vietnamese
Moderate

You can't miss this restaurant on the Nettle Bay road. Look for a pagoda with a large "garuda" (bird) over the front door. Buddhas and statues representing Thai gods are set in the beautifully landscaped gardens. The food served is Thai, Vietnamese and Japanese, and the menu has over 100 items from which to choose. There are fixed price menus as well. Japanese sashimi is excellent (the fish was caught just a few hours earlier). Other dishes include sugar cane-wrapped shrimp, steamed crabs with vermicelli, steamed fish curry with coconut milk and vermicelli with pork and shrimp. Meat dishes include Cantonese roast duck and sliced beef with mushrooms. There are many vegetarian dishes on the menu.

La Case Créole
Sandy Ground
☎ 590-87-28-45
Moderate
Creole

If you'd like to sample Creole specialties, this is a good place to start. In a colorful Creole house surrounded by a tropical garden, you can eat in one of two dining rooms. Each has pastel walls, red lacquered chairs and plaid tablecloths. The serving staff is dressed in traditional garb and the music sets the mood.

▣ TIP

One way to taste a lot of dishes is to order the Assiette Gourmande (Gourmet Platter), which includes grilled lobster, stuffed crab, Creole boudin, conch boudin, conch kebob, cod accras, shrimp accras, and stuffed Christophine. Side dishes include yam purée, giromen purée, plantains, red beans and Creole rice.

You can order such items as mango shrimp or conch with vanilla sauce from the à la carte menu. The restaurant opens at 6:30 pm and the dancing at the Hibiscus Club starts at 10 pm. Closed Sundays.

Le Mini-Club
Blvd. du Front de Mer
☎ 590-87-50-69
Creole
Inexpensive
Le Mini-Club looks like a giant tree house. Perched on thick wooden beams and set amid

towering palms, it is cooled by the breezes rolling in from Marigot Bay. It has weathered walls, a high beamed roof and lots of lush tropical plants to break the dining room into sections. Le Mini-Club was Marigot's first restaurant and remains a local favorite, especially on Wednesday and Saturday nights when they serve their Creole buffets. The long table is filled with lobsters, shrimp, and other seafood, and roasts of beef, lamb and pork are carved upon request. There are also salad fixings and fresh fruit. The price is right and it's very informal. There is an à la carte menu on other nights.

Sidewalk Cafés

Zee Best, Rue de la Liberté, is owned by a young French-Canadian couple. They make great sandwiches, breakfasts and salads. Take-out for picnics.

Le Colibre Patisserie, Rue de Gaulle, serves the most delicious pastries as well as sandwiches and salads.

La Pierrade, Port La Royale Marina, opens at 7 am for breakfast and doesn't close till midnight. Good light menu. Terrace tables.

Mentalo Snack Bar, Rue de Gaulle, serves burgers, sandwiches and pastries. In Le Village Arcade.

Chez Nini, Market Square, is just one of a cluster of small restaurants that line the square. They serve Creole food.

Panini, Port La Royale Marina, specializes in hero sandwiches on fresh Italian bread. Try a "Roma," with ham, brie and mushrooms, or a "Garibaldi," which has tuna, tomatoes and eggs. There are a half-dozen more and they serve good salads and desserts too. Good place for take-out.

Restaurants In Or Near Grand Case

La Rhumerie
Colombier
☎ 590-87-56-98
Gourmet French/Creole
Closed Thursday

Closed Sept. & Oct.

Expensive

La Rhumerie combines the best of St. Martin's French and Creole traditions. The result is gourmet Creole food. The restaurant itself is an attractive Creole cottage on a narrow road in Colombier, one of the most pastoral and traditional parts of the island. Since Creole cooking typically utilizes the freshest fish, produce and meats available, menus change daily.

There are several dining rooms, each with starchy white tablecloths, floral or plaid overlays and glossy chairs. A basket of freshly baked bread will appear on your table almost immediately. Starters could include cold cucumber soup or garlicky fisherman's soup. Other choices might be an avocado Creole-style or frog's legs Provençal. Main courses can include fish stew with curry, smoked chicken Guyana or conch or crayfish Creole. Leave room for the banana flambé or crème brûlée. Reservations are required.

> **回 TIP**
>
> Reservations are a must, so drive by the Rhumerie early in the day, check the menu and put your reservation under the door.

Le Tastevin

Blvd. de Grand Case
☎ 590-87-55-45
Lunch and dinner
Expensive-Very Expensive

The most elegant restaurant on the Grand Case strip, Le Tastevin is marked by striped green and white awnings. The tables, covered with deep blue tablecloths and encircled by high back rattan chairs, are set on the covered terrace on the beach side of the boulevard. There are beautiful flowers throughout, including some on each table. You can start light with a mixed salad with balsamic vinagrette dressing or the more filling lobster bisque. Main courses include fresh salmon with dill or grilled vegetables, seared tuna with pepper sauce or the duck breast with banana and lime sauce. Fabulous desserts include apple pie with red berry sauce and chocolate and praline mousse. Tastevin means "wine taster" and the wine list is terrific in a wide price range. Reservations for dinner are a must.

Fish Pot

Blvd. de Grand Case
☎ 590-87-50-88
Expensive
Dinner only. Closed Sunday

An elegant restaurant with a magnificent view of Grand Case Beach and the sparkling lights of Anguilla in the distance, Fish Pot is set on a long terrace and has a veranda right above the sand. Tables set with deep blue cloths and grey and apricot china are quite eyecatching. An imaginative menu features seafood (but also includes duck and veal). Fish Pot serves a delicious Caesar and brie salad and sautéed shrimp for openers. Lobster with ginger and lemon sauce has a unique taste, as does the blackened sea bass. Caribbean fish soup with big chunks of fish and shellfish is served as an appetizer and as a main course. If you eat lightly, you'll have room for the chocolate mousse cake or fruit tart.

Rainbow

Blvd. de Grand Case
☎ 590-87-55-80
Nouvelle French
Dinner only. Closed Sunday
Expensive

An attractive choice for dinner, Rainbow's split-level dining room with white beamed ceiling and walls, and blue and white checkered tablecloths, has a jaunty nautical look that is augmented by the sound of the waves just a few feet away. The menu at Rainbow is very innovative and has dishes not served elsewhere on the island. Among them is a shrimp and scallop fricassée, warm duck salad with fried onions, and bell peppers stuffed with lobster. You'll also find veal scallopini with capers and filet of red snapper with a parmesan crust. Great desserts include honey, orange and ginger soufflés and profiterols.

Il Nettuno

Blvd. de Grand Case
☎ 590-87-77-88
Moderate
Lunch noon to 3 pm; dinner 6 pm-10:30 pm

A delightful surprise on this street with so many French restaurants, Il Nettuno is an Italian establishment, and a very good one too. You'll notice the opera music as you step over the threshold. The green tiled bar is popular with people waiting for tables and others enjoying a drink at waterside. Graceful archways separate the bar area from the dining rooms where the tables are covered with pink cloths and floral napkins. A floral centerpiece marks the antipasto table that is covered with cheeses, marinated vegetables and cold meats. Start with the fiore de carpaccio salmon and calamari or the fresh mussels in a garlic tomato sauce. Homemade pasta, the house specialty, is served with a multitude of sauces. Ravioli with smoked salmon and veal scallopini with porcini mushrooms are customer favorites.

L'Auberge Gourmande

Blvd. de Grand Case
☎ 590-87-73-37
Moderate
Closed Wednesdays

The sturdy walls of this unusual stone *case* remained unscathed by the winds of Hurricane Luis. Not in typical Creole style, the house lacks a terrace and gingerbread trim, but instead has a covered stone patio and graceful archways that separate one dining area from the next. The frequently changing menu is primarily Nouvelle French. The evening specials are posted on a blackboard on the patio. Among the dishes often served are lamb chops with fine herbs, duck breast with honey and lemon, and chicken breast with apples. Other dishes include escargots and foie gras. This is an informal choice with unhurried service and a friendly staff.

Hevea

Blvd. de Grand Case
☎ 590-87-56-85   *Closed Sept.*
Expensive
Dinner Only

A tiny gem with less than a dozen tables, Hevea occupies the front rooms of a restored Creole mansion. Everything about the restaurant points to the owner's good taste. The walls are white and so are the hand-embroidered place mats at each setting. The floral china and plush red-cushioned armchairs give the dining areas a provincial look. The cuisine is delightfully French. Lobster bisque or grilled prawns are delicious starters. Main courses include duck with Madeira sauce, filet de boeuf in cognac, and the duet, which is mahi mahi and smoked salmon. Leave room for the banana flambé with rum or the chocolate delight with coffee cream. There is a pianist or a singer during dinner. Reservations are a must.

Le Pressoir

Blvd. de Grand Case
☎ 590-87-76-62
Moderate
French/Creole
Closed Tuesdays

One of the oldest Creole houses in Grand Case is home to Le Pressoir, a French restaurant with lots of Creole touches. Look for the iron "pressoir" at the door and park across the street. A pressoir would seem to be a tool used in printing. The dining rooms, separated by curved archways, have apricot walls trimmed with lavendar to match the wood beams on the ceiling and the window shutters. Tables covered with floral cloths add to the feeling that you're eating in a giant dollhouse. Don't miss the delicious onion-asparagus tart. Main courses include roast lamb with tropical fruit, sautéed sole with apples, pastas and roast duck. Desserts are a must here, with white chocolate mousse with cherries and hot chocolate mousse cake at the top of everyone's list.

The Lolos of Grand Case

"Lolos" were the beach shacks that once dotted Grand Case Beach. Typically made of wood with thatched roofs, they were no match for the winds of Hurricane Luis and many were not rebuilt after it hit. But a few more sturdy structures have reappeared here and on Friar's Beach nearby. Lolos serve barbecued spare ribs, chicken and lobster with johnnycakes, plantains and rice and beans. You can eat on the beach or take the food back to your room. It's finger lickin' good.

Eating with Kids on Grand Case

If your kids have had it with escargots and foie gras, head to the **Rock N' Roll Café**, a multi-level restaurant that shares Blvd. Grand Case with the gourmet restaurants detailed above.

Look for Mexican food, burgers, hot dogs and the works.

Dining Further North

Captain Oliver's
Oyster Pond
☎ 590-87-30-00
Moderate

Captain Oliver's resort sits on the French-Dutch border on beautiful Oyster Pond, a secluded cove on the island's eastern shore. In fact, the resort is on French soil, while the restaurant, built on wooden planks, is over Dutch waters. The terrace is open-sided but covered with white sail cloth and diners can watch the sailboats and yachts as they move through the canal to the marina. Capt. Oliver was a top restaurateur in Paris before building his hideaway here about 20 years ago. His goal here was to provide good food and good service at a moderate price. He has succeeded.

The restaurant opens from 7 am to 10:30 am for breakfast that includes a buffet. Reopening at noon, the lunch buffet and à la carte menu is served until 5 pm. The buffet has cold fish and meats, hot soups, salads and great desserts. Salads, burgers and sandwiches dominate the à la carte menu. At 5 pm the staff starts to set the tables for dinner with blue and white table cloths, lighted hurricane lamps, and more formal china and glassware. The dinner menu reflects Capt. Oliver's roots. It blends pastas and fried chicken with superbly cooked seafood, including lobsters from the tank prepared in a variety of ways. A cold appetizer called Ile Coco Cap't Oliver is sliced raw tuna in olive oil and a hot pepper sauce with coconut and lemon. It will please those who like sushi. Palm and avocado salad, stuffed crabs, Creole-style grouper and fine veal and duck dishes are other choices. The restaurant serves till 11 pm, although the bar stays open later.

Chez Yvette

Orleans, French Quarter
☎ 590-87-32-03
Inexpensive-Moderate

There are many family-run restaurants like Chez Yvette in the British Virgin Islands, but it is unique here. The restaurant, in a small white, pink and green *case* with gingerbread trim, sits in a small garden just off the main road in Orleans. Eating dinner here is like being invited to someone's home – only the food is better. There are only 10 tables, each one covered in a bright red cloth, with fresh flowers. Yvette, the owner and the chef, buys the freshest ingredients she can find each morning and then plans the menu. She and her staff cook "to the house," so you must have a reservation. The Creole dishes are prepared just as they would be in kitchens on the island. There is no overlay of French food. Yvette's favorites include salt fish cakes, spicy fish fritters (accras), spareribs, and conch and dumplings. Stews prepared with lobster, conch, chicken or pork chops are very popular. Vegetables and rice and peas are served with each main course. There are always soups and salads too. Yvette greets all her guests and is very friendly. Your evening here will be an enjoyable one.

L'Astrolabe
Esmeralda Resort
Orient Bay
☎ 590-87-36-36
Moderate
Closed Wednesdays

In its own building near the gate of this villa community, L'Astrolabe serves both breakfast and dinner. It is quite elegant inside, resembling a French restaurant in Nice, and has brown tile floors, pale posts that support the beamed ceiling (dividing the dining room into areas) and lots of prints and posters on the walls. The inner dining area is fan cooled and there are tables on the terrace as well. The terrace is in a garden setting in the rear of the house. Comfortable, it has high-backed armchairs and widely spaced tables set with fine crystal and china. The menu changes daily. A recent menu had sliced smoked salmon and lobster bisque for starters and many fish dishes, including jumbo shrimp with chutney and grilled mahi mahi with zucchini. The filet of beef with mushroom was served in puff pastry shell. There was a choice of desserts. Drive by early in the day or call to check on the menu before making reservations.

Dining In Or Near Philipsburg

L'Escargot
Front Street, Philipsburg
☎ 599-5-22483
Lunch and dinner
Expensive

It's a surprise to find that one of the island's top French restaurants is on the Dutch side of the island. But you know L'Escargot is first-rate because it's been here for over 25 years. You can't miss the landmark 19th-century house on Front Street that is painted in red, white and blue and has a long wrap-around veranda and lots of gingerbread trim. There are no subtle decorative touches inside either. The small dining areas have pink walls decorated with murals of France inspired by Toulouse Lautrec and lots of colorful posters. Other walls have hundreds of business cards from satisfied guests and requests for L'Escargot recipes. Escargots are the house specialty and are prepared with wild mushrooms and shallots, in cherry tomatoes and garlic butter, baked in garlic in pots or in an omelette. If snails aren't your favorite thing, you can start with frog's legs, crêpes filled with caviar or shrimp ravioli in lobster sauce. Main courses include shrimp in cognac and garlic butter, poached salmon in herb sauce or chicken breast with mango dressing. Crème brûlée and chocolate mousse are among the desserts.

Le Bec Fin

Front Street, Philipsburg
☎ 599-5-22976
Expensive

Walk through the flower-filled courtyard and up one level to the restaurant that offers classical French cuisine and great views of the bay through its galley windows. There are photos of Queen Beatrix of Holland when she supped here and other celebrity diners as well. Where L'Escargot is folksy, Le Bec Fin's decor is quite contemporary – mauve walls, dark carved wood chairs, hanging planters, and Colonial-style sconces providing indirect light. You'll soon notice shooting flames at neighboring tables. Grilled lobster tail flamed in cognac at your table is the most popular dish here. Other favorites are the shrimp and scallop kebabs with passion fruit sauce and the salmon and fishroll in sorrel sauce. Marinated rack of lamb and steak au poivre are long-time favorites. There is a prix-fixe menu each night. The garden-level Le Bec Fin Café serves breakfast and lunch. Stuffed crêpes top the menu.

The Wajang Doll

Front Street, Philipsburg
☎ 599-5-22687
Moderate
Dinner only, 7 pm to 10 pm
Closed Sundays

While there are no Dutch restaurants on St. Maarten, there are a number of Indonesian (formerly Dutch East Indies) restaurants that serve the traditional *rijsttafel*. Translated as "rice table," it is an Indonesian smorgasbord that starts with rice and 20 or more dishes eaten with it. Dishes include meats, vegetables and fruits. The à la carte menu includes *saté udang*, which is marinated shrimp kebabs with peanut sauce, and *sup jawa*, a soup with rice noodles and spicy meatballs. A *wajang doll* is a prop used in Indonesian folklore plays. Ask for a table in the garden of this brown and yellow West Indian house that is near Old Street.

Old Captain

Front Street, Philipsburg
☎ 599-5-26988
Moderate
An island of Chinese and Japanese fare in a sea of French restaurants, Old Captain is an attractive port of call. Its pink and black onyx dining room with colorful aquariums and its narrow terrace offer a respite from bustling Front Street. The sushi bar is the restaurant's most popular stop. And why not? The yellowtail tuna and wahoo came from this morning's catch. They and other fish are served as sushi, sashimi, temaki and norimake. Other Japanese foods, such as tepanyaki with beef, chicken and shrimp, are also served. The large Chinese menu includes stirfries, curries and lots of vegetarian dishes.

Ric's Place
Front Street, Philipsburg
☎ 599-5-26050
Inexpensive

The island's only real sports bar (you can watch U.S. sporting events at some of the casinos), Ric's looks like a bar in a college town. Its walls are decorated with pennants of sports teams — both professional and college. There are several TV sets and when events aren't on live, they show videos of games. Hot dogs, burgers, meatball grinders, burritos and chicken wings are all easily washed down with a draught beer. They have Fosters, Bass and over a dozen others from Holland, Germany and England. Wood tables scarred by cigarette burns and people leaving their names for posterity are scattered on the tile floor. Ric's sits right on the beach.

Spartaco
Almond Grove, Cole Bay
☎ 599-5-45379
Expensive

Floodlights allow this beautiful 200-year-old stone plantation house to shine even at night. The restored estate has magnificent gardens with palm trees, flowering plants and marble statues. Spartaco serves Northern Italian food and imports many of the ingredients from Italy. All the pastas and the olive oil is made in-house. House specialties include grilled radicchio in onion and caper vinaigrette, mussels sautéed in garlic and black angel hair pasta sautéed with shrimp and artichoke. Veal Vesuviana, with mozzarella and tomatoes and rack of lamb are good choices. Tiramisu and terrine of chocolate are great finishers but you might prefer dessert and after dinner drinks in the Spartaco Cigar Bar where jazz and classical music is live from 11 pm to 2 am.

Mark's Place
Food Center, Cole Bay
☎ 599-5-32625
Inexpensive-Moderate
Lunch and dinner
Closed Sunday and Monday

We remembered Mark's Place from previous trips to St. Martin when it was an informal bistro on the Orient Beach Road. It was not there when we returned for this book, but we were delighted to stumble over it in its new location near Spartaco Restaurant. Still informal and still serving huge portions of Creole specialties and fresh seafood, it seems to be going strong. Daily specials are posted on the blackboard.

Dining In Or Near Maho

La Rosa Too
Maho Village
☎ 599-5-53470
Moderate
Dinner only, till 11 pm
Closed Tuesday

In a quiet corner of the Maho Complex, La Rosa Too's customers are primarily people who live or winter on the island. Table-talk, all in English, revolves around golf scores, bridge games and the latest gossip. The owners are very gregarious and very welcoming – and the kitchen prepares delicious Italian dishes. The menu is very large and items are prepared to order so be prepared to have a drink at the bar while waiting for your table. Starters include beef and salmon carpaccio and steamed clams, and there are lots of pasta dishes which can be ordered in half-portions. Chicken is prepared piccata and parmigiana, veal comes milanese style or with peppers and the osso bucco comes with gnocchi. There are small dining areas set off by glass walls. Tables can be close when the restaurant is crowded.

Le Bistrot Gourmand
Cupecoy Bay
☎ 599-5-52429
Moderate
This is a delightful choice in an area where there are few restaurants. It is located in a small shopping arcade near the entrance to the beach. The indoor dining room has weathered wicker chairs, green and white cloths and very nice works of art. There are a few terrace tables as well. Marinated salmon Scandinavian-style or a leafy green salad are good starters. If you like pasta, there are several on the menu and always some specials. Tuna steak Cajun-style, chicken piccata with capers, and mixed seafood

with saffron rice are all delicious. If you still have room, try the apple crêpe with honey or the chocolate profiteroles. Reservations are a must.

Cheri's Café
Maho Village
No Reservations
Inexpensive-Moderate

Informal and with lots of options, Cheri's Café is the busiest restaurant on the island – French or Dutch. An open-sided, roof-covered, circular terrace is set with umbrella-covered tables and multi-colored director's chairs. Cheri's opens for lunch at 11 am and serves till midnight. The live music starts at 8 pm. Salads come with tuna, sardines or turkey and the burgers with cheese, onion or bacon. There are super-size sandwiches and spaghetti with meat, shrimp or garlic butter sauce. You can eat light, but there's also steak and shrimp or steak and lobster combos, tuna and shrimp brochettes and pasta specials, like lasagne. There is a kids menu for those under 12. No credit cards.

Dining in Simpson Bay

Lynette's
Airport Road, Simpson Bay
☎ 599-5-52865
Inexpensive-Moderate

Lynette's Creole restaurant sits near the runway at Princess Juliana Airport. The outside,
marked by a neon sign, is drab, but the dining
room sparkles. It has rust tile floors offset by
pastel walls with lots of gingerbread trim and
widely spaced tables encircled by peacock rattan chairs. But it is the grilled fish and lobster,
the fabulous ribs and all the fixings that bring
locals and island visitors to this small restaurant. There is a Lynette and she is highly visible, making sure that everyone feels right at
home. Save some room for the bananas Foster
(flamed bananas in island rum with vanilla ice
cream). Lynette's is also open for lunch.

回 *TIP*

Make reservations for dinner
on Tuesdays and Fridays and
stay for the Calypso show, often
featuring King Beau Beau.

Sambuca Ristorante

Simpson Bay
☎ 599-5-52633
Inexpensive

Offering a happy mix of Italian and American
specialties, Sambuca is an attractive restaurant on Airport Road. The street is lined with
fast food eateries, but an all-stone exterior and
a bright cheery interior make Sambuca a step
up from its neighbors. The bar is a popular
hangout. Pizzas, baked in a wood-burning oven,
are served with sausage, pepperoni, seafood or
peppers. Other Italian dishes include lasagne,

canneloni and fettucini primavera. If you prefer American dishes, try the sirloin steak, the roast chicken or the barbecued spare ribs. Be adventurous and order a "bucket of dirt" for dessert. Dinner from 6 pm. Sunday brunch. Lunch.

The Boathouse Restaurant
Simpson Bay
☎ 599-5-45409
Inexpensive

An anchored boat decorated with flags and mermaids at Simpson Bay Lagoon serves as The Boathouse Restaurant. The rectangular bar is a popular local hangout and is quite crowded at happy hour. Since The Boathouse serves breakfast, lunch and dinner, it is always bustling. You can enjoy eggs, pancakes and omelettes at breakfast (7:30 to 10:30 am), followed by salads, sandwiches, burgers and pastas for lunch (11:30 am to 2:30 pm). Dinner, which is served until 10 pm, has a conch cocktail or peel n' eat shrimp, seafood kebabs, surf n' turf, and filet mignon. Friday evenings a rock group entertains. You can head to the adjacent News Café after dinner. No breakfast or lunch is served on Sundays.

★ NOTE

Chesterfields, Great Bay Marina, Philipsburg, has the same menu, same ambience and same owners.

After Dark

The days are hardly long enough to squeeze in all the things you want to do, so after-dark action on the island is low key and filled with very good food, island music, piano bars, theme nights and casino chips. Check the newspaper or ask your concierge about events during your stay. Always call clubs before starting out. Hot spots never last long.

Maho Plaza

A lively nighttime destination with a score of restaurants, a casino, comedy club and theater. **Cheri's Café**, a covered terrace restaurant, has live music every night from 8 pm to 1 am. You can have just drinks or dine there. **Coconuts Comedy Club** (in the Casino Royale Building) has both local and imported talent. **La Luna Discotheque** is open nightly at 10 pm in high season with only weekend hours off-season. The shops here stay open late as well.

Marigot

Head to **Port La Royale**, where the walkways adjoining the marina house a dozen restaurants – some gourmet and some informal – serving everything from French food to pizza. All the restaurants have indoor and terrace dining and menus are posted. They are crowded well into the night. We've detailed some of the restaurants above, but you can come for a nightcap and the live music too. Another nighttime center, **Market Square**, is two blocks away, on the dock. There are some gourmet restaurants here, but there are many more informal cafés with patios that serve Creole food, including barbecued ribs and chicken. There's live calypso and reggae music nightly in the plaza.

Arawak Café is also popular.

The most popular café, **Le Bar de La Mer**, doesn't take reservations, so expect to wait for a table. **La Vie en Rose** at the edge of the plaza has a sidewalk café where they serve French pastries long after the restaurant has closed. **L'Aventure**, near Fort Marigot, is a popular discotheque. It's open weekends and draws a European crowd. Informal, funky attire. ☎ 590-87-13-85.

Orient Beach

Popular during the day, the beachfront restaurants here are also open and alive well into the night. Informal but not shacks, these restaurants have both indoor and outdoor dining areas. The diners are a good mix of locals and visitors, and the restaurants are noisy and full of fun. The food served varies from Spanish tapas to pizza to French fare. Check posted menus. Bikini Beach, Kakao, Kon-Tiki, Coco Beach and Waikiki each has a private parking area. You can walk from one to the other.

Reservations are not necessary at the beach places.

Le Privilège Hotel and Spa

On a hilltop overlooking Marcel Cove (about 20 minutes from Marigot), this hotel is active every night. The **Panoramic Restaurant** serves nouvelle French foods each night, but most people wait for the theme nights, which are wild. Usually on Fridays, the guests and even the staff take part. Past themes include Brazilian Nights, Circus Nights, and Transvestite Nights. It's a hoot. There is live music with dinner on Wednesday through Sunday. A discotheque opens on the grounds in high season. Call ahead to find out what's happening. ☎ 590-87-38-38.

Casinos

All the casinos on the island are on the Dutch side of the border. Most are in hotel complexes, but there are a few in Philipsburg too. They all have slot machines, blackjack, roulette and craps. Some have stud poker, while others offer betting on horseraces and sports events. They include: **Casino Royale** (Maho), **Lightning** (Simpson Bay), **Rouge et Noir** and the **Coliseum** (both on Front Street, Philipsburg), **Great Bay Casino** (Great Bay Hotel, Philipsburg), **Pelican Casino** (Pelican Hotel, Simpson Bay), **Atlantis Casino** (Cupecoy Bay)

Must be 18 years old to gamble.

Calypso/Reggae

Lynette's Restaurant-Airport Road, ☎ 599-5-52865. Creole food. St. Martin's most popular calypso singer, King Beau-Beau, sings here. Friday nights 8 pm (more often high-season).

Pub 1950's-Amsterdam Shopping Center, Madame Estate, ☎ 599-5-25482. Serves Creole and American food and features local bands, calypso, reggae and karaoke.

Piano Bars

You can enjoy the background music during and after dinner at some of the island's finest resorts.

La Samanna (☎ 590-87-64-00), **Panoramic Privilege** (☎ 590-87-38-38), **La Belle Créole** (☎ 590-87-66-00), **Oyster Bay Beach Hotel** (☎ 599-5-22206).

Jazz & Other Music

Spartaco Cigar Bar, Almond Grove Bay (☎ 599-5-45379), features jazz, popular and classical music along with fine wines, cognacs and cigars. Music from 11 pm. The **Spartaco Italian Restaurant** is set in a restored plantation house built in 1795.

The Greenhouse, Bobby's Marina, Philipsburg (☎ 599-5-22941) has informal menu and live music.

New Music Café, Simpson Bay (☎ 599-5-42236) has several levels. One is a discotheque and the other has big screen TV and pool tables.

Casablanca, Great Bay Beach Hotel (☎ 599-5-22446), a nightclub adjoining the casino, has live music every night. Local bands and others from the Caribbean.

***Lady Mary* Cruise**, Palapa Center, Airport Road (☎ 599-5-53892). This 85-foot yacht cruises for 14 miles around Simpson Lagoon. Creole food, fine wines and champagnes are served. Special theme cruises include Brazilian Night (with live entertainment), Champagne Cruises (steel bands) and Late Night Party Cruises (DJ and dancing). All good fun.

Carré Club, Auberge de Mer, Marigot (☎ 590-87-55-07), is a "private club" that will admit tourists (or anyone with enough francs) to its dimly lit night. Comfortable black leather couches, DJ and mostly male clientele. Closed Monday. Hours are 7 pm till 2:30 am.

L'Hibiscus Club, La Case Creole, Sandy Ground (☎ 590-87-28-45), opens at 10 pm every night but Monday. They have jazz and Brazilian nights, Caribbean music on Wednesdays and a show on weekends.

St. Martin A to Z

Banks

Chase Manhattan, Philipsburg and Simpson Bay. Hours: 8:30 am-3 pm, Monday through Friday.

Banque des Antilles Françaises (BDAF), Marigot. Hours: 8 am to noon and 2 to 3:30 pm, Monday through Friday.

Climate

Sunny and warm year-round. Average temperature is 80°F. Constant trade winds moderate the temperature.

Clothing

Informal is the key word. Casual chic attire is the norm at the better restaurants, but shorts are accepted in the casinos and moderate restaurants. Jackets are rare. No ties.

Currency Exchange

Change Caraïbes-Rue de Général de Gaulle, Marigot.

Departure Tax

Passengers departing on international flights from Princess Juliana Airport must pay a $12 departure tax. The inter-island departure tax is $5. All taxes are included in the ticket price on the French side.

Electric Current

Dutch Side-110V, the same as in the United States. No convertors or adapters are required.

French Side-220V. Requires a convertor and French adapter plug.

Emergency Numbers

French Side: **Police**, ☎ 87-88-33; **Hospital**, ☎ 29-57-57.

Dutch Side: **Police**, ☎ 22222; **Hospital**, ☎ 31111.

Holidays

Contact tourist offices, listed below, for details.

January 6 - **Epiphany** (French side). Dining, dancing and observing ancient French custom of serving "galette des rois" (King's Cake).

February (date varies) - French **Carnival** is a pre-Lenten celebration that lasts till Ash Wednesday. Parties, parades and a Carnival Queen are part of the celebration.

March (date varies) - Sint Maarten's **Heineken Regatta** is a well-attended sailing race with entrants from all over the Caribbean.

April (date varies) - The Dutch **Carnival** celebration lasts two weeks. A Carnival King and Queen are elected and there are parades. Events are held at the Carnival Village in Philipsburg.

May 30 - Dutch Sint Maarten celebrates the **Queen's birthday** with fireworks.

July 14 - French St. Martin celebrates **Bastille Day** (Independence Day) with parades and fireworks.

November 11 - **St. Martin's Day** celebrates the signing of the treaty that divided the island with ceremonies held at the marker on Terres Basses/Cupecoy Beach.

Marinas

French Side - **Captain Oliver's**, Oyster Road, ☎ 87-33-47; **Port de Lonvilliers**, Anse Marcel, ☎ 87-31-94.

Dutch Side - **Bobby's Marina**, Philipsburg, ☎ 22366; **Simpson Bay Yacht Club**, Simpson Bay, ☎ 43378.

Mini-Golf

There is bowling and a mini-golf course at the **Howell Center** in Marigot. Hours: 10 am to 10 pm, Monday through Saturday.

Newspapers

The *Miami Herald* and *USA Today* are sold in Maho Bay.

You'll also find *The News,* in French, and *The Herald*, in English.

Personal Safety

Use the same common sense you would at home.

- ⊚ Don't flash money or wear expensive jewelry.
- ⊚ Avoid areas that are dark after business hours.
- ⊚ Do not leave valuables in your car overnight, even if the car is locked.
- ⊚ Lock your car at the beach.

Photo Express

In front of Hotel Marina Royale, Marigot. ☎ 87-07-27.

Prescription Drugs

Bring enough drugs to last your entire trip. Over the counter items are readily available.

Physicians

Should you need a doctor, ask your concierge to recommend one or to contact one for you. There are dentists and doctors with a wide variety of specialties on the island.

Population

There are approximately 30,000 people living in Saint Martin and 33,000 in Sint Maarten.

Post Office

Dutch Side - Philipsburg.

French Side - Marigot, Grand Case, Orléans.

Religious Institutions

There are Anglican, Baptist, Catholic, Latter Day Saints, Methodists, Jehovah's Witnesses and Seventh Day Adventist churches (with some on both sides of the island). Jewish services are held during the High Holy Days.

Time Zone

When the eastern coast of the United States is in Eastern Standard Time, the time in St. Martin is plus one hour. During Daylight Savings Time, the times are exactly the same. The French side uses the 24-hour clock.

Telephones

Area Codes: French St. Martin, 590; Dutch Sint Maarten, 5995.

On-Island Calls: To call the French side from the Dutch side, dial 06 + six-digit number.

To call the Dutch side from the French side, dial 195995 + five-digit number.

Credit Card Calls from public phones. From the French side, dial 19-00-11 (requires deposit). From the Dutch side, dial 001-800-872-2881. You will be connected to AT&T.

Local Calls from Public Phones: French St. Martin requires a France Telecom Card that can be purchased in a post office. No coins are accepted.

Dutch Sint Maarten requires a Netherlands Antilles Telecom Card, which you can buy at the post office.

Tourist Offices

St. Martin: Bureau d'Office du Tourism, Marigot Port, ☎ 590-87-57-23. Hours: Monday through Friday, 8:30 am to 1 pm and 2:30 to 5:30 pm. Saturday, 8 am to 12 noon.

Sint Maarten: Wathy Square, near pier. ☎ 599-5-22337. Hours: Monday through Saturday, 8 am to 12 noon, 1 to 5 pm.

Anguilla

A Daytrip Or Weekend Getaway

Eating dinner at a restaurant in Marigot's Market Square or in one along Grand Case Beach, you'll notice twinkling lights on the horizon. It's Anguilla, five miles north of St. Martin and the most northerly of the Leeward Islands. One of the few islands not named by Columbus, Anguilla is 16 miles long and three miles wide. The long narrow shape may be responsible for its name; "anguilla" is the French word for eel. Only slightly smaller than St. Martin/Sint Maarten, Anguilla has only 10,000 citizens. The island is quite flat. Its highest point is Crocus Hill, 213 feet above sea level. It is also very dry and, like St. Barts, it has no rivers or streams. This made it difficult to grow sugar or cotton, so the few plantations that were built failed and few slaves were brought to Anguilla.

The earliest colonists were British, from St. Christopher (St. Kitts), 70 miles southeast. St. Kitts was Britain's most important colony in the Caribbean. Anguilla was twice attacked by the French – the last time in 1796 – but English frigates arrived in time to defend the island. In 1688, a group of Irish sailors came to the island. Their descendants are clustered in Island Harbour. The island's population is predominantly of African descent. Without agriculture, Anguillans turned to the sea and eked out livings as fishermen and boat-builders.

★ DID YOU KNOW?

The island's national sport is not cricket but boat racing.

An incident in the 1960's brought Anguilla onto the world scene. In a situation that parallels an early Peter Seller's movie, *The Mouse that Roared*, British paratroopers landed on Anguilla to prevent it from withdrawing from the Associated State Britain had established with Nevis and St. Kitts. Anguilla was an unwilling participant. In February 1967, Anguilla evicted the St. Kittian police and set up its own government on Anguilla Day, May 30. The British sent an advisor to try and resolve the situation, but when he was unable to do so, the British Red Devils invaded the island. It took 10 more years for Anguilla to formally separate from St. Kitts-Nevis, but it remains an Associated State. It has a British Governor as well as a locally elected legislature.

The premise of *The Mouse that Roared* was that after a war Britain always rebuilds and enhances the vanquished country – and that is what happened here. New roads were built, as was the airport, and lots of long-overdue projects were completed.

As TV news broadcasts covered this "invasion," they showed the island and its world-class beaches. The tourist industry was born.

Anguilla's beaches are stunning. It has elegant resorts and over 50 good restaurants. It is a laid-back, informal destination and great for a honeymoon.

The Beaches

Anguilla's beaches are truly prize-winning. There are dozens of them and they are covered with beautiful, white sand. Fronted by clear blue waters, the beaches are crescent-shaped and run as far as the eye can see. Some are backed by limestone cliffs, others have seagrape trees and waterfront centers. Still others house elegant resorts and restaurants. Many have coral reefs near the shore so snorkeling is easy and fun. Looking at a map of the island, you'll notice the overwhelming number of places that are bays, points and harbors.

Shoal Bay East

This may be the best beach in the Caribbean. It stretches for a mile, has very clear water and a coral reef very near the shore. Hotels and restaurants are on the beach. Watersports and lounge chair rentals are offered.

Island Harbour Bay

Lined by coconut trees, this is home base for the brightly colored motor-powered fishing boats that bring in the day's catch of lobster and fish. There are restaurants here. Take the three-minute boat ride to Scilly Bay for snorkeling and lunch.

Rendezvous Bay

This 1½-mile beach has calm waters and is home to the Sonesta Beach Resort and smaller hotels and restaurants.

Barnes Bay

Cliffs line the bay and you'll have to climb down to the beach. The coral reef is close enough to the shore that you can see the multi-colored fish darting through it. This is a great windsurfing beach. Watersports rentals and restaurants are offered.

Maundy's Bay

This popular beach is home to Cap Juluca Resort (featured in *Lifestyles of the Rich and Famous*). It is over one mile long. There's no coral reef here, but the beach is good for swimming and watersports (rentals available). Restaurant.

Shoal Bay West End

From Shoal Bay you can see St. Martin and the cruise ships in the distance. Snorkeling is excellent. Fishermen set nets on one end of the beach. Stop for conch fritters at the Paradise Café.

Road Bay

(also called Sandy Ground)

Lots of yachts and sailboats anchor here. It is an excellent windsurfing and waterskiing beach. Watersports rentals.

Watersports

Scuba Diving

Scuba diving is well organized and the island offers both natural and man-made sites. They include coral fields, shipwrecks, underwater canyons, and cliff edges. Dives include night and photographic tours.

Anguillan Divers	☎ 809-497-4750
Dive Shop	☎ 809-497-2020

Horseback Riding

A daily trail ride is offered at **El Rancho del Blues**, ☎ 809-497-6164.

Tennis

Peter Burwash International manages tennis programs throughout the Caribbean. Here it manages **Cap Juluca's** three courts and **Malliouhana's** four courts. There are courts at the **Sonesta Beach Resort, Cinnamon Reef Beach Club** and the **Fountain Beach and Tennis Club**.

Day Sails

Sails to a deserted cay or secluded beach are offered by the following:

Wildcat Services	☎ 497-2665
Sandy Island Enterprises	☎ 497-6395

Sunup to Sundown

Sightseeing

The Valley

Mid-island, The Valley is Anguilla's capital. Wallblake Airport is on the outskirts of the town, as is the old salt pond. The town has a half-dozen streets, schools, churches, local businesses and shops. In town sights include:

Wallblake House: Built in 1787 with stone cut on the island's East End. It's a traditional plantation house with carved woodwork in its ceilings. The grounds have a cistern and a "bakery" that baked meats. It's owned by the Catholic Church and services are held on the grounds.

Old Island House: A two-story wooden structure built in 1800. Renovated by a local family and painted apple green, it once housed magistrates but is now an art gallery.

Old Warden's Place: The traditional home of the island administrator and doctor is now a restaurant. The stone work here is impressive.

The Old Factory: Opposite Wallblake House, the factory produced island gin. It was originally part of the plantation.

Around The Island

Sand Hill: There is an old fort here that the island defenders took refuge in when the French attacked in 1796.

Island Harbor: A quaint fishing village where many people have Irish ancestors. The brightly painted boats often go 40 or 50 miles offshore to bring in lobsters and fish. A small museum about the Amerindians who lived on the island is on the grounds of the Arawak Beach Resort.

Crocus Hill Prison: On the island's highest point at 213 feet, the prison is in ruins but the view is fabulous.

Best Places to Stay

Resorts

Sonesta Anguilla Beach Resort
☎ (800) 766-3782; fax (305) 670-0040
Expensive
Formerly the Casablanca Hotel, the Sonesta mixes white marble and colorful mosaics, Moroccan arches and tropical gardens. Its beach runs for three miles, and it has a magnificent pool, fitness center, and tennis courts. Several restaurants.

Cap Juluca
☎ (800) 323-0139; fax (212) 363-8044
Deluxe
Cap Jaluca offers white moorish buildings along a two-mile beach. Accommodations include rooms, suites and villas. The resort has two restaurants, tennis courts, watersports center and fitness room.

Malliouhana
☎ (800) 835-0796; fax (809) 497-6011
Deluxe
This is stunning building with boutiques and restaurants sits on a hillside overlooking two beaches. Watersports center, two swimming pools, tennis and fitness center.

Tourist Board Information

There are many hotels and guest houses on the island. Information is available from the tourist board.

Anguilla Tourist Board, ☎ (809) 497-2759

In the United States, ☎ (800) 553-4939; fax (305) 670-0040.

Best Places to Eat

Blanchards'
Meads Bay
☎ (809) 497-6100
Expensive

On the waterfront, Blanchards' serves Cajun, Caribbean and Asian specialties. Extensive wine cellar. Dinner only.

Arlo's Place
South Hill
☎ (809) 497-6810
Expensive

Italian food, with the island's best pizza. Dinner only.

Paradise Café
Shoal Bay West
☎ (809) 497-6010
Inexpensive

A beachfront restaurant that serves food from burgers to bouillabaisse to pizzas.

Ferryboat Inn
Blowing Point
☎ (809) 497-6613
Expensive
Near the ferry dock, this is a French restaurant serving lobster thermidor and steak au poivre. The onion and black bean soups are house specialties.

Hibernia
Island Harbour
☎ (809) 497-4290
Moderate
The chef studied in Bangkok and many specialties are Southeast Asian. Others are French and include duck and local seafood.

Uncle Ernie's
Shoal Bay
Inexpensive
A local hangout with inexpensive beer, Creole food and live music on weekends. Open 10 am to 8 pm.

Getting There

By Boat

Ferries leave from the pier in Marigot for the 20-minute crossing to Blowing Point, Anguilla every half-hour starting at 8 am. The last ferry leaves at 5:30 pm. Return ferries leave from 8:30 am until 5 pm. Late night ferries leave Marigot at 7 pm and 11 pm and Blowing Point at 6 pm and 9:15 pm. The fare is $10 each way and there is a $2 departure tax. Proof of citizenship is required.

By Air

You can fly into Princess Juliana Airport, Sint Maarten and connect to a commuter line for the seven-minute flight to Wallblake Airport. Winair, Air Anguilla and LIAT make this flight several times daily in season.

You can also fly to Puerto Rico and connect to American Eagle for the one-hour connecting flight.

Getting Around

Day-Trippers: A private taxi island tour costs $40.

Bicycles: Rent a bicycle at Blowing Point Ferry Terminal.

Car Rentals: Drive on the left.

Thrifty	☎ (809) 497-2656
Island	☎ (809) 497-2723
Hertz	☎ (809) 497-2934
Connors	☎ (809) 497-6433

Taxis: Taxis meet flights and ferries. There are no meters, but there is a flat, fixed rate.

Index

Other Books In This Series

CANCUN & COZUMEL ALIVE
328 pages $15.95   1-55650-830-1

ARUBA, BONAIRE & CURAÇAO ALIVE
304 pages $15.95   1-55650-756-9

BUENOS AIRES & THE BEST OF ARGENTINA ALIVE
424 pages $15.95   1-55650-680-5

VENEZUELA ALIVE
384 pages $15.95   1-55650-800-X

THE VIRGIN ISLANDS ALIVE
400 pages $15.95   1-55650-711-9

All Hunter titles are available at bookstores nationwide or from publisher. To order direct, ☎ 800-255-0343 or send a check plus $3 shipping and handling per book to Hunter Publishing, 130 Campus Drive, Edison, NJ 08818. Secure credit card orders may be made at the Hunter website, where you'll also find in-depth descriptions of the hundreds of travel guides from Hunter. Visit us at www.hunterpublishing.com.

Adventure Guides™

This signature Hunter series targets travelers eager to really explore the destination, not just visit it. Extensively researched and offering the very latest information available, *Adventure Guides* are written by knowledgeable, experienced authors, often local residents.

Adventure Guides offer the best mix of conventional travel guide and high adventure book. They cover all the basics every traveler needs – where to stay and eat, sightseeing, transportation, climate, culural issues, geography, when to go and other practicalities – followed by the adventures. Whether your idea of "adventure" is parasailing, hiking, swimming, horseback riding, hang-gliding, skiing, beachcombing or rock climbing, these books have all the information you need. The best local outfitters are listed, along with contact information. Valuable tips from the authors will save you money, headaches and hassle.

Town and regional maps make navigation easy. Photos complement the lively text. All *Adventure Guides* are fully indexed.

Adventure Guide to the Alaska Highway

Adventure Guide to Arizona

Adventure Guide to the Bahamas

Adventure Guide to Barbados

Explore Belize

Adventure Guide to Bermuda

Adventure Guide to Canada's Atlantic Provinces

Adventure Guide to the Catskills & Adirondacks

Adventure Guide to the Cayman Islands

Adventure Guide to Colorado

Adventure Guide to Costa Rica

Explore the Dominican Republic

Adventure Guide to the Florida Keys & Everglades National Park

Adventure Guide to Georgia

Adventure Guide to the Georgia & Carolina Coasts

Adventure Guide to the Great Smoky Mountains

Adventure Guide to Hawaii

Adventure Guide to the High Southwest

Adventure Guide to Idaho

Adventure Guide to Jamaica

Adventure Guide to the Leeward Islands

Adventure Guide to Michigan

Adventure Guide to Nevada

Adventure Guide to New Hampshire

Adventure Guide to New Mexico

Adventure Guide to Northern California

Adventure Guide to Northern Florida
& the Panhandle

Adventure Guide to Oklahoma

Adventure Guide to Oregon & Washinton

Adventure Guide to Orlando & Central Florida

Adventure Guide to the Pacific Northwest

Adevnture Guide to Puerto Rico

Adventure Guide to the Sierra Nevada

Adventure Guide to Southeast Florida

Adventure Guide to Southern California

Adventure Guide to Tennessee

Adventure Guide to Texas

Adventure Guide to Trinidad & Tobago

Adventure Guide to Utah

Adventure Guide to Vermont

Adventure Guide to the Virgin Islands

Adventure Guide to Virginia

Adventure Guide to the Yucatán